My Incredible Journey With Roger

To order additional copies of
My Incredible Journey With Roger, by Hilda Morneau,
call **1-800-765-6955**.

Visit us at

www.reviewandherald.com

for information on other Review and Herald® products.

How beautiful on the mountains
are the feet of the messenger who brings good news,
the good news of peace and salvation,
the news that the God of Israel reigns!

ISAIAH 52:7, NLT

HILDA MORNEAU

REVIEW AND HERALD® PUBLISHING ASSOCIATION
Since 1861 | www.reviewandherald.com

Review and Herald® titles may be purchased in bulk for educational, business, fund-raising, or sales promotional use. For information, e-mail SpecialMarkets@reviewandherald.com.

The Review and Herald® Publishing Association publishes biblically based materials for spiritual, physical, and mental growth and Christian discipleship.

The author assumes full responsibility for the accuracy of all facts and quotations as cited in this book.

Scripture quotations marked NLT are taken from the *Holy Bible,* New Living Translation, copyright © 1996. Used by permission of Tyndale House Publishers, Inc., Wheaton, Illinois 60189. All rights reserved.

Bible texts credited to KJV are from the King James Version of the Bible.

Bible texts credited to NRSV are from the New Revised Standard Version of the Bible, copyright © 1989 by the Division of Christian Education of the National Council of the Churches of Christ in the U.S.A. Used by permission.

This book was
Edited by Penny Estes Wheeler
Cover designed by Matthew Pierce/PierceCreative.com
Cover photos © 2010 iStock
Typeset: Bembo 12/14

PRINTED IN U.S.A.
15 14 13 12 11   5 4 3 2 1

Library of Congress Cataloging-in-Publication Data
Morneau, Hilda, 1926-   .
  My Incredible Journey With Roger / Hilda Morneau.
     p. cm.
  Includes bibliographical references.
  1. Morneau, Hilda, 1926- 2. Morneau, Roger J., 1925- 3. Seventh-day Adventists—Canada—Biography. 4. Seventh-day Adventists—United States—Biography. I. Title.
  BX6193.M677A3 2011
  286.7'32092—dc22
  [B]
                                        2010011260

ISBN 978-0-8280-2498-3

Dedication

These reflections are dedicated to the memory
of my husband, Roger, my one true love.
He kept my heart and life filled with a
sincere appreciation of God's unconditional
love for all His created beings.
Roger truly was a dedicated servant of God.

Acknowledgments

S ome days I would be amused at how this book was falling into place. Certainly God has a great sense of humor to put into my mind that I could provide a part of the history of the Canadian colporteur work as well as the prayer ministries through a book that is merely recollections from my childhood to old age. But the years of accumulating notes, photos, papers, and letters paid off when I needed names and exact dates. Roger so laughed over my scrapbooks!

Many people have dramatically touched my life. Gerald Wheeler from the Review and Herald Publishing Association planted the seed for this book with the encouragement of Penny, his wife. These two were responsible for Roger being in print from his first, *Trip Into the Supernatural*, to the three-book series, *Incredible Answers to Prayer*, to his last, *Beware of Angels*. The Review and Herald's book acquisitions editor, Jeannette Johnson, repeatedly helped me understand more of what was needed for the manuscript, while both Gerald and Penny Wheeler answered many questions about the translation of Roger's books into other languages, and other nuts and bolts of further printings. As for this project, there are not enough words to express how much I appreciate the patience and endless energy of Neilann Martinez as she typed out my life's journey.

Within this life sketch, names are mentioned in their context, and to each person I send my heartfelt appreciation for their being such an important part of our lives. In addition, I think of a couple, who now rest in Jesus, whose names are not in the book, yet who meant so much to us. They are Richard and Marie Lukens, and their encouragement to me and Roger was always timely and immeasurable.

After Roger's death, I placed all the cards and letters I received into five scrapbooks. Let me just add how thankful I was and am for all the people who reached out to me when I needed comfort. My heart goes out to all who have lost loved ones. It is a painful time. Many notes shared how Roger touched their lives. I am grateful that others were able to be blessed, as I was, to have known Roger. We had been together for 51 years plus two days—September 20, 1947, to September 22, 1998.

Years have now passed, yet letters still come, requesting prayer for increased faith and a need to have a closer relationship with their God. We can all be assured that God hears such cries for help and is answering those heartfelt prayers.

Our adult children, Donald, Linda, and Daniel, "rolled up their sleeves" and did hundreds of things that encouraged and helped us, making our lives more comfortable. And even more so now, as I live without Roger, I have had their faithful love and care. In my older years I lean mainly on Linda and her dear husband, Michael. There are no words to express my appreciation for each of our children and the love I have for my grandchildren and great-grandchildren.

Last and most, the One to thank is God who many years ago brought Grace Villaneuve into my life. A sweet, young Christian mother, in 1944 Grace shared her love for Jesus with me. Where did she receive such love? The Holy Bible revealed the Messiah, the Son of Man, the Son of God. His Word and the Holy Spirit transforms sinners like me, like Grace. From what we learn of God, we know He is the One we want to be around, to be like Him. What love is this, that on the cross He thought of me?

Contents

Chapter 1   Canada and the Early Years 11

Chapter 2   Our Broken Family 20

Chapter 3   Truth Versus Tradition 25

Chapter 4   Making a Living 31

Chapter 5   "Bob" 34

Chapter 6   Out of Darkness Into Light 38

Chapter 7   A Small Home Wedding 40

Chapter 8   Mac and Cheese—Everywhere 43

Chapter 9   Depending on the Lord 48

Chapter 10   The Monsigneur's Photo 51

Chapter 11   Two Wheels for Four 55

Chapter 12   Moving On 58

Chapter 13   The Years Slip By 75

Chapter 14   Scary Times, Happy Times 84

Chapter 15   God's Light Still Shines 88

Chapter 16   Roger's First Heart Attack 95

Chapter 17   Gift of Time for Mother 100

Chapter 18   Two Phone Calls 105

Chapter 19   California, Here We Come! 107

Chapter 20   The Impact of *Incredible Answers to Prayer* 119

Chapter 21   Dark Day 122

Chapter 22   The Years Without Roger 125

chapter 1

CANADA AND THE EARLY YEARS

What makes a prayer warrior? What led Roger and I to so deeply love the Lord?

Dwight Nelson, a leading minister of the Seventh-day Adventist Church called Roger Morneau a prayer warrior." And now, as Roger's widow, I have been asked to write about his and my life. But I ponder, what led us to deeply love the Lord and long for everyone to be brought to the experience of having an intimate life with God for themselves? Both Roger and I were steeped in Catholicism. That spiritual background gave us a reverence for God and life in a culture that came with being part of faithful Catholic families. How could we leave the Catholic traditions and set out on a course marked by only faith in God as defined by the Bible? To this end, I will continue on, tracing steps that brought both Roger and I to love God more than life itself. With God is the never-ending intimate friendship that leaves out none of our earthly Christian friends. Dear Reader, if you will, set out with me as I tell of the ways God led Roger and me.

Where to begin? I guess the only place is to begin at the very beginning. I was born June 15, 1926, in the little town of Ansonville, in the province of Ontario, into a strong Catholic family where there was love, nurturing, and plenty of singing and music. I weighed 10 pounds at birth, a breach birth to a very small mother. The doctor used forceps to help the delivery, causing permanent injury to my right arm in what is called today Herpes Palsy, where the nerve endings are pulled off the muscles.

At 8:00 a.m. on May 25, 1925, on a typically cold and snowy day, my mother, Mary Ann (Annie) Le Claire, married my father, Raphael Simon Mousseau. The wedding was held in a very small town in Northern Ontario called Iroquois Falls. A few friends and family gathered at the Catholic Church for their short ceremony. My maternal grandmother had not been dead quite a year, therefore, no reception was celebrated. Mom and Dad left the church to catch the train for Timmins for a short honeymoon. Dad was employed by the Abitibi Paper Company and because he was not eligible for vacation time, they could not have a long honeymoon.

Dad was 22 and Mom was 17. The future looked bright, and their dreams were high. They loved one another dearly, and they believed that they could take whatever the future held. Mama was a beautiful woman, five-foot-two with eyes of blue, fair skinned with natural curly hair, and Dad was tall, dark, and handsome, always singing or humming a happy tune. I arrived on a beautiful Tuesday morning, born at home. My parents did everything possible to bring me up unspoiled, but because I was their only child, this may be debatable by some. Mom and Dad showed by their example that unless you could share whatever you had with someone else— whether food, candy, toys, anything—you would not bring them out for yourself only. You went without.

My early memories of Mom and Dad are very happy ones. They both loved sports. They played hockey, ice skated indoors and out, enjoyed tobogganing, bobsledding, Taffy pulls, and popping corn in a wire basket over a wood-burning kitchen stove. In later years, Dad not only was president of the Quebec-Montmorency Hockey League, the Mount Ste Anne Ski Club, the local softball league—he formed the first local union of papermakers as well.

At Christmas, Mom and Dad would pack me in a sleigh with gifts all around me. Then they pulled the sleigh across the crunched snow covering the wooden sidewalks. We were delivering Christmas presents, mostly handmade or hand knitted, to aunts and uncles and many cousins. All the children looked forward to Aunt Annie's delicious, homemade candy, cookies, and candied apples. Though these were very happy memories, I won't ever forget the Christmas we had delivered gifts to our wonderful family when, going home, Dad tripped and fell over a black metal pipe sticking out of the sidewalk. He was in such excruciating pain that he had to climb into the sleigh with me, and Mom pulled us the rest of the way home. I was too young to later recall exactly what kept him laid up for weeks, but Dad had to stay home to get better.

It seemed to me that in Ansonville, the little town where I was born, everyone was related. In those days many children blessed each home. When summer came, we spent a lot of time at the different nearby lakes. Both Mom and Dad were expert swimmers, and Dad was a lifeguard. I personally witnessed him save people from drowning. He was born in Fort Coulonge, Province Quebec. His family lived across the road from the Ottawa River, so all of them learned to swim at an early age. In fact, everyone who lived near the river learned to swim young. Swimming was second nature to all the young lads in his day.

I always thought our summers at the lake with friends and family were the best times of my childhood. Berries were plentiful, and we all pitched in picking. I especially remember the blueberries because they were my favorite. Of course, we kids ate even more berries than filled our small pails. Then there was Dad's way of baking beans in the sand. He had a big, black iron pot, and in it went the beans, liquid, and seasonings. Then he'd put on the heavy iron lid and wrap the pot in newspapers. He'd dig a big hole in the sand, place the pot in the hole, and cover it with sand. Then he built a bonfire on the sand over the pot. All night long Dad fed the fire with the sticks we children had gathered, so the beans baked all night, and were ready to be eaten the next day. That was Dad's job, baking the beans, and he loved doing it!

Dad loved to tell stories around the bonfire, especially wild scary animal stories. He made the sounds and noises. Afterward, we kids always had a hard time going to sleep for we'd hear a twig crackle and be sure it was a bear coming to get us.

Mom and Dad liked to sing together. Mom sang a little off key, while Dad had a strong tenor voice. I will always remember the joy of hearing them sing. Too, they loved to dance around the house. Dad would jig, and we would clap our hands to cheer him on.

Dad's side of the family was very musical. One of my great-uncles, Euchere Mousseau, played the fiddle by ear, and he and my aunt had a large family—seven girls and one boy. They all played musical instruments—piano, organ, all types of stringed instruments, and harmonica. They also had beautiful singing voices. How they entertained the family and friends for many happy evenings! There was no place for loneliness then.

My father's mother, Mary, played the organ beautifully for him and his siblings. And when I visited, she would play just for me. Grandma Mary was the kindest and sweetest grandma you could ever wish to have. Always happy, I saw tears only when we arrived for a visit and when we left. She worked so hard to make sure that her family would enjoy their stay. Though she was up early in the morning until late at night, she always had time to give me hugs and kisses and to tell me what a good girl I was. I was her only grandchild for 16 years. Grandma had eight children, and my dad was the oldest. He married several years before any of the other children did.

My grandfather, Euchere Mousseau, was the town clerk. Later, he was mayor of Fort Coulonge for many years. He enjoyed politics and followed all the elections. As a small child, I remember that a Mr. McDonald was running for some political office in Fort Coulonge, and Grandpa wanted him elected, so the whole family got involved in promoting him. Lots of cheering and marching went on. Grandpa was away from home a great deal so I never got to know him as well as I did my grandma. Grandma Mousseau was typical for those years—short and chunky. I would watch Grandma chop the head off of the chicken that we were going to eat, and she'd hear my cries of "Don't do it!" She'd sorrowfully explain that she had to as Grandpa was not there, and the family needed to eat. It was always hard for me to eat after that.

My mother's father, Le Clair, was very upset that my parents married before Mother's mother had been dead a year. Grandfather Le Clair did not like my father to begin with. At one time he'd been a neighbor to the Mousseaus in Fort Coulonge. He never got along with the Mousseaus, so when my mother married Raphael

Mousseau, he was very unhappy. Grandpa Le Clair told them that he would not attend their wedding, but when they walked out of the church they saw Grandpa sitting in his work clothes in the very last pew.

Mom and Dad found lodging in Ansonville, the same town where Grandpa Le Clair lived, and when he got quite ill he came and asked Mother if they would consider living with him. I was still very young then, around age 3 or 4. Grandpa needed my parents' help, and it was a good thing for our family, too. Grandpa had one of the nicest homes in Ansonville. He'd built it himself and it had two stories and a summer kitchen. It was easily large enough to accommodate our small family as well as him.

Grandpa had lost his hand at the paper mill, and he wore a hook. I was about 4 when he scared me so badly that I never wanted to be around him. It was because I aggravated him by going around the house looking for my mother and calling "Mama, where are you?" Grandpa called me over to him and grabbed my left wrist with his hook arm, and shook it harshly. He held me by the hook, looking right at my face, and I could not get away. I cried, of course.

Mother came, and Grandpa let go, and Mother told me to come with her, quieting me. She then explained that Grandpa was sick, and that was why he shook me. She told me to stay away from Grandpa—something I did not need to be told. I truly did not want to go near him again.

It was while in Pembroke to visit his dying sister in the hospital that Grandpa Le Clair himself died. My Uncle John, my mother's brother—the oldest son—had come from Quebec City to be with Grandpa as he visited his sister. But then Grandpa became critically ill and was also hospitalized. Soon Uncle John had to return to his job in

Quebec City, so he contacted Mother and told her that Grandpa was gravely ill. Of course, Mother hurried to Pembroke to be with Grandpa, leaving me in Ansonville with one of her sisters, my Aunt Josie. She had to take me to school, as I was in the first grade. Aunt Josie lived in a different part of town than where we lived, and things were so strange to me. It seemed to me that Mother was gone forever. I cried for her every day.

My parents lived in Grandpa's house for a few more years, then they decided to sell the house and move to Iroquois Falls which was approximately three miles from Ansonville. Most of the town was owned by the Abitibi Paper Company who rented homes to the workers there. The company house our family rented needed repair, but there were some fun things about it too. Attached to the house was a huge woodshed for storing the wood used during the winter. There was a lot of room in the shed, and my dad put a large swing in there for me. Sometimes Mother and I would swing on it together. A window in the kitchen looked into the shed, and she could look out and see if I was alright when I played out there alone. We had a large kitchen and a lovely large living room. From the living room a beautiful winding staircase rose to the second floor. My room was at the end of the hall above the kitchen.

That was such a happy home. Mom and Dad worked tirelessly, wallpapering the kitchen and putting down new linoleum. All the rest of the house had hardwood floors. The wood was very dark on both the banister and the floors, but when the black was cleaned away we discovered that the wood was actually golden. It was just beautiful. The living room was underneath my mom and dad's bedroom. They called it a bungalow. I remember Dad shopping and buying a new style of heating system. It was run with an oil-based liquid in a stove that opened where we could view the flames. It had a pipe that took the smoke outside.

Dad had a large garden at the back of the house. Even though we had a very short summer season, he was able to grow potatoes, tomatoes, cucumbers, string beans, and radishes. When he wasn't at work, he spent most of his time in the garden. Mother could not even go out to the garden, for it was *his* garden. I soon learned the hard way about that.

I had a wonderful friend named Lillian Parron who lived two houses from me. We must have been around 9 years old when we were crazy about cutout paper dolls. In town was a company ice cream parlor that sold homemade ice cream, sundaes, milk shakes, candy, magazines, and newspapers. Every month when a new shipment of magazines came in, Lillian and I would borrow her brother's wagon and head for the ice cream parlor. We weren't going for ice cream or candy. Instead, we'd hurry to the back of the parlor where all the old newspapers and magazines had been put. We'd load up the wagon, haul it to my house, and bring everything up to my bedroom. There had to be two of everything we chose, one for Lillian and one for me. If there was only one picture of Shirley Temple, for example, we'd almost have a scrap over it. Of course, Mother heard us. Once when she came up and opened my door, she nearly fell over when she saw papers covering my bed and the entire room. Lillian was crying. I told Mother that Lillian had the picture of Shirley Temple and would not let me have it.

Mother said to Lillian, "You take the picture and all the other pictures, and now you go home. Hilda and I are going to have quite a talk." This happened not once, but many times. The funniest part was that Lillian would go home crying, telling her mother how "mean Hilda is." The first thing you'd know, Mrs. Parron was at Mother's door trying to find out just what happened. Mother would tell me just what she had told Mrs. Parron. I recall Mother saying, "Don't worry. In an hour, they'll be back together." And we were.

Lillian loved their family's wonderful two-seated lawn swing, and she often sang as we swung. She had long dark hair and blue eyes. She was truly beautiful. I was very blond.

Shortly after Dad and Mom had the house fixed like they'd dreamed it would be, we had the joy of having Grandma Mousseau come and visit. Mostly she stayed with her daughter, Aunt Edna, who lived in Ansonville. When Aunt Edna had her first pregnancy, it was Grandma who came to be of help to her, but Aunt Edna did not understand that and wouldn't let her do anything for her. When Grandma came to visit us, staying a few days or a week, she asked my mother, "Would I be able to wash your floor?"

Mother set Grandma up with what was needed, and she washed the floor. How pleased Grandma was to be of help. She was so happy to do it that she told my father, "Annie let me wash the floor today."

chapter 2

OUR BROKEN FAMILY

I was 11 years old in 1937, when the Abitibi Paper Company in Iroquois Falls transferred Dad and seven other families to Beaupré, a small town in the province of Quebec, on the shores of the St. Lawrence River approximately 20 miles east of Quebec City. I had a very difficult time in my new school for they used the French language and we spoke English in our home. Many of my cousins, aunts, and uncles spoke French so I could speak and understand it, but I could not read it nor write it.

This was a very difficult move for my parents. My mother was quite concerned over the amount of liquor and bootlegging in Quebec as three of her brothers had lived for several years in Quebec City and she knew all about their lifestyles. It would be so different from the way we had lived in Iroquois Falls. Two of the brothers had become very serious drinkers. Mother planned to send me to an English convent, The Immaculate Conception, as I was running around on my bike and she was very concerned that I would fall into bad hands.

At this time war broke out between Germany and England, and the paper mill was working only two or three days per week. It was then my own father began to drink heavily and did not come home on many a night. It was the beginning of our family breaking up. When war was declared, I was in a Catholic convent boarding school in Pembroke, Ontario, about 20 miles from the home of my grandparents, my father's family. I spent all school holidays with my grandparents in Fort Coulonge.

Then since Dad was not working, and things were not good at home between him and my mother, she wrote a letter to the Sisters in the convent, telling them that I must come home and asking them to pack my things and use the money she'd enclosed for train fare to buy my ticket. I was 15, and in the ninth grade, and had been at the convent for just a few months when the letter arrived. I boarded the train dressed in the convent uniform—black stockings, black shoes, and a black dress that stopped just a little above my ankles. The dress had a large, stiff white collar and white cuffs. I will always remember the clothing. I had liked the sisters and the convent lifestyle. Surely if I had stayed, I would have become a nun.

After I was home, most probably a few weeks, I told Mom that I needed to find work. All the young people that were too young to be in the military were working. It was a serious time of war. Mom took me to Jeffrey Hale Hospital, the only English hospital in Quebec City. You had to be 16 to work there as a nurse's aide, and they were about to dismiss me when Mother spoke up. "She's going to be 16 in June," she said. "Can you make an exception?"

Even though my birthday wasn't for another six months, the Director of Nurses said that she could, and asked Mom, "Do you think she is mature enough for the maternity floor?"

"Oh, yes!" Mother replied.

I had worked a year at the hospital, where I had room and board, when someone called and told me that Mom's and Dad's house had burned, and that Mother said that I had to come home to Beaupré. The fire—electrical—started in my bedroom closet. The paper company had an inn which had been built especially for employees who came from their own home area to work at the Beaupré Abitibi Paper Mill. It was both a place for them to lodge while working at the mill and for administrative staff to stay when overseeing the mill's operation.

The manager of the inn had quit, and the Abitibi owner asked my dad if he'd be willing to manage the staff house while his own house was being rebuilt. Dad agreed, and that was when life got really, really difficult. My dad started drinking more and having affairs with some of the women on the staff. Then Mother got seriously ill. She was trying to be a cook, which was quite a big job and more than she could handle. One of my dad's brothers, Uncle John Mousseau, was a cook in the Abitibi Lumber Camps. Dad, Uncle John's eldest brother, asked him to come and help with the cooking at the Staff House, which he did.

Those years were very hard, not for just our family, but for many. I had to come back from Jeffrey Hale Hospital to help out at the Inn. My folks asked me to wait on tables, but my right arm disability made it too difficult to carry trays, so I went to work in the laundry room that was in the basement.

During this difficult time, Mom was admitted to the hospital. By now I was 17 years old, and so attached to my mother that the nuns let me stay near her in one of their rooms.

Mom was in Saint-Anne Hospital in Ste. Anne de Beaupré, where people knew that healings took place. Prayers for nine consecutive days, called novena were and still are offered there. Because some patients experienced miraculous healing there, people came from all over the world. It started as a place of healing centuries ago when fishermen, out in the St. Lawrence River, did not think they would make it to shore. They prayed to Sainte-Anne, and said if they got safely to shore, they would have a chapel built there. Ste. Anne was supposedly the mother of Mary the mother of Jesus. The fishermen did survive and landed there. They kept their vow, building the chapel that was a duplicate of the one in Rome. It later became a large church. Novenas are still being made.

Mom was not healed, but she got better and went to live for a few weeks with a friend in Ste. Anne de Beaupré. She did not go back to live with my father.

But I remember something very kind my father did for his parents. When my grandma and grandfather celebrated their fiftieth wedding anniversary, my father purchased a new yellow Chrysler convertible, especially to get his mom and dad and take them on a trip from Fort Coulonge to Niagara Falls. They had never gone on a trip together before this. The Catholic Church made a celebration of their fiftieth wedding anniversary with a mass and reception at the church hall. Grandma looked so sweet. By now my parents had separated. The church did not accept divorce, but would allow for separation.

After leaving my mother's friends, we left to go to Montreal. I did the packing, not sure of what I was doing or if I was doing it well. We took the train to Montreal, and when we arrived I was surprised to see that my father's brother, Uncle John, came to meet us. Mother had not told me that we would be staying with him. He took us to his private apartment, owned by a Protestant pastor. The apartment was only one room—for all three of us. This is how we began life in Montreal.

The next morning I was in tears in the living room when the father of the landlord, now a retired pastor, came into the room. He wondered why I was crying. I told him that I needed to find a job and the only thing I knew was how to be a nurse's aide. He looked in the newspaper to see if he could find something for me, and saw that the Shriners Crippled Children's Hospital had an ad for nurse's aides. He told me how to get there by streetcar and bus. The Director of Nurses, Miss Ore, who interviewed me, said that she had room and board and uniforms.

"When could you begin?" she asked.

I said, "Right Away."

She hoped I would not mind sharing one large room with two other girls, and I didn't care. When I got to the hospital, I met Isabel Robinson who was hired the very same day. But she would not live there as I did. This was the Isabel who introduced me to her sister who later had given me Bible studies.

Uncle John and my mother went to the woods as cooks for the lumber camp, and were gone all winter. When Mother returned to Montreal and was living in a different section of the city, she finally made the decision to leave Uncle John. By then I was working at a city hospital, because Shriners Hospital had been downsized. It was called the Infirmary, and was an old people's home, large, dark, and depressing. Rows and rows of beds were lined side by side in these long rooms. There might be 20 to 30 patients in the long rows. The women were placed in one section and the men in another. I often worked at night, and found it very fearful. These dear people often got out of bed and walked those dim rooms and halls at night, and we had to get them back to their beds. It was not an easy task. I was probably 20 years old.

chapter 3

TRUTH VERSUS TRADITION

Montreal is that beautiful city in Quebec Province where thousands of French and English people live, the city where my precious Savior found me in the year 1944. Yes, I was one of his lost sheep, but not knowing I was lost, until a precious Christian came into my life. Grace Villeneuve, was Isabel's sister. She attended the Westmount Seventh-day Adventist Church. Praise the Lord that by His Holy Spirit, she was able to share the love of her God with me, resulting in my conversion to the truths of God's Holy Word. The errors that were revealed of my Catholic faith cut deeply into my heart for I loved my church and was not looking for a different faith.

Grace became a dear, dear friend. She was such a loving and caring person that it was difficult for me to believe that she was not Catholic. Yet many times when I left Grace, I would promise myself that I would not return to visit her, for the pain our conversations inflicted on my heart was unbearable. Never having had a Bible, I was in a state of shock in regard to many Catholic teachings—the doctrine of the Mass, Confession, Peter as the Rock and founder of God's church, what happens after death, and most shocking, the changing of the Ten Commandments. It all was so overwhelming that tears flowed easily when I left the Villeneuve's home.

I met Grace through her sister Isabel who was one of my coworkers. She had invited me to a young people's social that Grace was going to attend. Isabel knew it would be a fun occasion for me to meet her sister, and Grace and I hit it off from the first. After the social, she invited me to come over to her home at any time. We talked, and she gave me her phone number and said, "Just give me a call." So began our friendship.

On my days off, I loved to visit Grace and her two precious children, a boy and a girl. I came to love them very much. But Grace was my first Protestant friend, and I simply had a difficult time understanding how she was not a Catholic. She was such a good person, even better than most Catholics. I never heard her swear, whereas every second word I said was "God." "God" this, or "God" that, until one day Grace said, "Hilda, do you realize how often you use the name of God?"

That really stunned me for I truly had not noticed. How God had to work on me for me to change. As most of you know, in the past Catholics had very little connection with Protestants. As small children, we were taught that all Protestants were a lost people in God's eyes, just like the Jews, and we Catholics needed to be on guard against them. We must not listen to them, attend any of their services, or even enter into their churches.

But Grace talked so plainly about the Bible and the love she had for God and Jesus. I truly could not believe my ears. There were times when I would promise myself that I would not return to visit Grace, but God's plan for me was different.

Grace would say, "You know, Hilda, when you leave here, I always ask God to send His Holy Spirit with you so you will remember the things we have talked about."

"And so do I pray," I'd tell her, "except that *I* ask God to help me *forget* the things we've talked about, especially the things about my church and its teachings." Our tears were often shed together as the Holy Spirit worked with my conscience. But you know, the more I prayed to *not* remember the new things I heard, the deeper they were implanted in my soul and I hungered for more.

With a great deal of prayer, I had a onetime Bible study with the pastor of the Seventh-day Adventist French Mission, Andre Rochat. He clearly explained the impossibility of Peter being the Rock, for it would be Jesus and He only who could be the Rock. I remember that he asked, "Hilda, what are the things you are hearing that you would like explained?"

I answered, "Peter as the Rock."

And he turned to the Bible and read some verses to me, and then so gently asked me, "Hilda, who do you think God would build the church on? Would it be Peter or Christ?"

"It would be Christ," I replied, for there was no other answer.

I also had questions about mass, confession, and communion, and Pastor Rochat answered them from the Bible. He stressed that Jesus would not be re-created, and have us eat His body and drink His blood literally, but that He gave the wine and bread as a symbol, a re-membrance of His body and blood offered as a sacrifice for all sinners who repented of their sins. Another important truth I learned was to confess my sins to God personally, instead of confessing to another human being, and that by this repentant prayer and faith in God's promise, I am forgiven. I cried when I finally realized how great a Savior I had. Today my heart still beats quickly when I recall the joy of knowing I have such a loving Savior.

Mother came back into my life after about a year had passed, and I was studying with Grace and Pastor Rochat. I visited her and Uncle John in Montreal and told Mother that I had made the decision to leave the Catholic Church. She was so angry that she said, "You are not a daughter of mine!" We lost contact for a month or so.

Then my mother left my uncle. What is amazing is that Mother found a place to live on the very street where Grace lived. When I learned of it, I could hardly believe it. I had room and board at the infirmary. The fact that Mother reached me at Grace's was nearly impossible, yet I was there as she phoned, and she asked me to come and spend the night with her on my day off. So I did. The apartments of Grace and Mother were where the municipal library was located at the beginning of the street and ran into Sherbrooke Boulevard (one of the largest streets in Montreal). When I stayed overnight with Mother she told me she was sorry and cried over the many things she had done that were not right. She asked if she could come and work where I was. Not only did Mother find work there, but for many years her supervisor was one of her best friends.

Whenever I wanted a friend, I would go down the hill to Grace's house. As she lived only a few doors from her, Mother did not say anything at all. I liked going to Grace's because it was always so wonderful to be there with her and her family. One day I ran down the outside staircase, along the sidewalk. It was spring and warm, yet with snow still on the walkway. Grace was coming up the sidewalk with her two children, one in each hand. "Where are you going?" I asked.

And she said, "Why, Hilda, this is Sabbath. We are going to church."

I said, "Will you wait? I'll go to church with you."

Of course, she said, "Yes" and was beaming with joy. I was wearing slacks so ran back to Mom's and changed my clothes.

That day's church service had a life changing message for me, as Pastor Phillip Moores preached on the second commandment. It was painful to hear, for it is the second commandment that explains the biblical view of making images and bowing down to them. Visiting there, I was amazed at the humility I found in the church. It did not draw attention to the church building, but drew attention to the message that is found in the sermons and songs. I was so impressed with the caring of the congregation, their friendliness, and understanding of the Bible's teachings.

Sometimes while Grace was sharing these beautiful truths with me, her husband, Armond, would be in the bedroom with the door open. Every now and again, he'd call out a comment such as, "Don't listen to her, Hilda, she's crazy. When it comes to religion, she's plain crazy!" But some years later, he, a faithful Catholic, turned around and become a "crazy" person too!

On April 1, 1999, I contacted Grace to request permission to include the above anecdote in the book I was writing, and she gave her consent. Then she shared with me memories from before I came into her life. Because she was a busy mom with two small children, she could see no way to share her love for the Lord, yet she longed to do so. So Grace kept praying that God would bring someone into her life with whom she could share the Word of God. When I began to show interest in her and her family and to come to her home, she knew that God had heard her prayer, and I was that answer.

May God bless each one of His children that has such a desire to share His Word. Surely "His word is not returned unto Him void" (see Isaiah 55:11).

Between my studies with the pastor and Grace's friendship, I committed to be baptized by immersion, the Lord's way. It was 1946, and I was baptized at the Westmount Seventh-day Adventist Church by Pastor Andre Le Coutre who worked for the Ontario-Quebec Conference. Praise God, the Holy Spirit was able to bring such conviction into my life. To Him I will be ever thankful, and to my dearest friend, Grace, for she was the one who first opened the Word of God for me.

chapter 4

MAKING A LIVING

The summer of 1946 I did canvassing, selling Seventh-day Adventist books door-to-door in Cornwall, Ontario Province, along the St. Lawrence River. Mother came to visit me and was looking for work. She made friends with the woman who owned the room I was renting, and when she and I went back to Montreal, they kept in touch.

Shortly after I canvassed I had an appendicitis attack and was rushed into emergency surgery. Mother, a nursing aide, was working at the hospital that day. She notified my dad, and he came to visit me. It was the first time I had seen him since I left Beaupré in October, 1944. Dad paid my doctor and the hospital expenses. I remember it so clearly, as though it were yesterday. He brought me flowers too. But my heart was so cold toward him for all the heartache he had caused both Mother and me. May the good Lord forgive me for my cold heartedness for I know God does not reward us with what *we* deserve.

Out of the hospital and convalescing, I was able to return to Montreal with Mother within a couple of weeks. The woman in Cornwall, who had become friends with Mother, wrote that she was expecting a baby and wondered if Mom would come and help her after the baby's birth. Mother decided to do that. Through this relationship, Mother learned that the woman had a first cousin, Mrs. Boidman, who lived in Montreal.

The Boidman's owned a large factory there; in fact, they owned a couple factories that made women's clothes and hats. As Mrs. Boidman was involved in the family's business—she was the overseer of the stores that they owned on St. Catherine Street—they were looking for someone to be a live-in nanny for their 3-year-old son. In Montreal the business owners were mostly Jewish, and Mr. and Mrs. Boidman were themselves Jewish. They had a large apartment in the city, on Queen Mary Road, and Mother joined them there. They were expecting a new baby, and she treated those two little ones—the little boy and baby girl—like her own children. The Boidmans just loved her, and Mother was very good to them as well.

She sewed for the children, making the little boy his trousers, and outfits for both children, which endeared her to the family even more. Mother was a true seamstress, and made all my clothes until I was 17. Now she poured the same love and skill she'd given me into the Boidman children.

Now that I was back in Montreal it was good to see Grace again, but I found her packing to move to Oshawa. I was very upset and asked her why they were moving there. Grace said, "Well, Hilda, there's not a church school in Montreal that will teach in English, but there's a church school in Oshawa that does. Too, Armond can find work at our church's publishing house."

Armond was accepted for a job in the bindery of the publishing company, even though they did not normally hire people who were not Seventh-day Adventists. He continued for years to believe and practice his Catholic faith even as he worked for the Adventist publishing house. Then one day he became a different man—as vocal as Grace had been, and still was, about the good news of Jesus in the Scriptures and in his own life.

The seed for me to train to be an LPN (Licensed Practical Nurse) was planted by my mother when she left aide work and went to be with the Boidmans. She offered to financially help me get through the training. So I gladly took the course at the Montreal Convalescent Hospital. A part of the requirement was to give a year's service to that hospital after I graduated. It was during this time when Bob came into my life.

chapter 5

"BOB"

Both Roger and I will treasure forever the way the dear Lord brought us together. Roger was baptized in March 1947, and we were frequently brought together by our pastor, L.W. Taylor, when we went out to distribute Voice of Prophecy pamphlets house-to-house. These were invitations for people to listen to the Voice of Prophecy radio broadcast, and to take Bible studies. Somehow Roger and I were always teamed together, either driven to the pick-up station on St. Catherine Street, Montreal, or passing out Voice of Prophecy pamphlets on Sabbath afternoons. Sometimes we were the only two left to catch our streetcars home. So Roger would suggest that we would walk together, talking about all the truths we had learned and loved.

One Sunday, while I was on duty at Montreal Convalescent Hospital, I received a phone call. I had not been to church for a couple of Sabbaths. I wasn't used to getting calls at my job, so thought the call must be something about my mother. But it was Roger. His voice was so low, I could barely hear him, so I asked, "Is this Bob?"

"Yes," he said.

For some reason I thought his name was Robert, so I called him Bob, and he answered to it. From then on, he was "Bob." One day I finally asked him why his friends, Cynthia and Cyril, called him Roger.

"That's my name," he told me.

"Well, why didn't you tell me that your name wasn't Bob?" I asked him.

His answer was unbelievable. "Well, you see, I thought it was an English nickname for someone you liked." We both had a great laugh. And Roger was "Bob" for many years, and my family referred to him for many years as Bob. In fact, if he had not published his books, to all his family and friends he most probably would have always been just plain Bob. But praise the Lord, by whatever name he was known, he gave a great many people hope in a Savior.

Back to the phone call. Roger was asking me for a date!

You know what my answer would be to Roger's question: Would you be off next Sunday?

Of course, it was, Yes.

We met the next Sunday and walked and visited St. Joseph's Shrine on Queen Mary Road. The shrine was just across the road from where I lived. And we went to the beautiful wax museum, which is where Roger wanted to go. It was in the museum that Roger first held my hand and my whole world suddenly turned around. What a gift God has given to man and woman to fall in love. I couldn't wait for weekends when I wasn't working so I could spend time with him. He was the most caring and polite person I had ever met.

However . . . he did have one very sad fault, and it was difficult for me to understand at first. He never was on time. No matter what time he'd tell me that he'd be at my place to pick me up, he was always late.

Mother would say, "Hilda why don't you just leave, and he won't find you here when he comes." But I did not have the heart to do this, for dear Roger would always have a good reason or explanation for being late. Either he'd spent most of the night reading Scripture or he would have started studying in the morning and didn't check the time until it was later than he realized.

Of course, after watching streetcar after streetcar come and go from my fourth-floor window, without his being on one of them, it was very tempting to follow Mother's advice. But the joy Roger showed when he was finally with me erased all my bad feelings, and he never forgot to ask for my forgiveness.

Then came that special evening in midsummer when he asked me the big question: "Will you marry me?" I didn't even need to think about it. He was the best and greatest thing that had ever happened to me. I was in seventh heaven, as we used to say. I got right on the phone and called my mother to tell her the wonderful news. Of course this was too soon for her to accept.

"I do not know this boy, and you probably do not know that much about him yourself," was her response.

I was simply crushed to say the least, and shed many tears. Why couldn't she see how happy I was and how much I loved him?

Mother was not the only one upset with Roger and my relationship. I worked at the convalescent hospital and slept there during most of our courtship. The building had a night watchman and when I'd arrive I would ring the bell for him to come and let me into the complex. But it always took a while, and it would seem he wasn't coming. When he finally came, he was very unhappy because Roger would give me another last-minute kiss.

"Oh, you girls!" he'd sputter. "When are you going to learn to come in before the door is locked? I am at the other end of the building, and I still have to wait for you to have that last good night kiss."

He was so angry this particular night, but I quickly shared, "Yes, but it's not every night a man asks a girl to marry him."

Needless to say, Roger and I started as friends and soon became sweethearts. And we remained sweethearts all our lives.

chapter 6

OUT OF DARKNESS INTO LIGHT

Before Roger and I were married, we talked over the difficult paths we had traveled in life before we had met. We made certain vows together, as all engaged couples do. Some seemed easy enough, but others may have been more difficult. When Roger tried to explain to me how deeply he had been involved in the supernatural world and demon worship, his words did not open my understanding to the depths that he had gone into that world. My exposure to it was as simplistic as watching a magician's illusions or a carnival fortune teller. I knew very little of actual demon worship—only a few stories I'd heard of how some heathens worshipped someplace very far away. However, the deep emotion Roger showed as he told just part of his experience with the supernatural world was overwhelming. He cried so uncontrollably that I held him tightly in my arms, crying along with him. I asked God to bring peace into his life as well as into mine.

I said, "Darling, you know that Jesus loves us both dearly to have brought us both out of darkness into this perfect light. We know that our past has been cast into the deepest seas, never to be remembered. What is important right now is that we both desire to follow Christ, to seek His guidance for the rest of our journey and His righteousness, by God's grace, which will sustain us, because we believe in God the Father, the Son, and the Holy Ghost."

And so both Roger and I vowed that we would never talk of this again, not even to our children, should we be so blessed. But God had other plans.

Those of you who have read Roger's books and have seen the videos he made, know the things that took place after 1984, when Roger nearly died during his first bout with congestive heart failure. It was after that that he first wrote about his experience with demon worship, the effect it had on his life, and how God literally saved his life from Satan's power. Sometimes human vows are changed by God's infinite wisdom so that others may be blessed and kept from being deceived, even as Roger had been deceived. Indeed this was the case, as many, many people were blessed by his testimony.

Often the people who read Roger's books asked how he could have such an intensely close relationship with God. But could it be that his experience was similar to what Jesus spoke about when He was on earth regarding those who have been forgiven much? Of the woman who washed His feet with perfume, Jesus said, "Her sins, which were many, have been forgiven; hence, she has shown great love. But the one to whom little is forgiven, loves little" (Luke 7:47, NRSV).

Luke 7:50 concludes the story of how this woman demonstrated her gratitude to her loving Savior, and His response. When others condemned her actions, Jesus said to her, "Thy faith hath saved thee; go in peace" (KJV). Roger, too, was in peace as he walked with his God. May this be our experience also. What a loving Savior! We are so unworthy, but He believes in us, and though we are unworthy He has paid the price to save us.

chapter 7

A Small
Home Wedding

Once Mother accepted the fact that Roger and I were going to be married, she did everything that she could possibly do to be sure that I had a nice trousseau. The Boidmans gave Mother a tremendous discount for clothing sold at their store. I remember the beautiful suit I wore for our wedding.

Our wedding took place after Sabbath, September 20, 1947, in Art and Ruth Cheeseman's home. Such a coincidence, for this home was the very first Adventist home I'd been in and it was where I first met Adventists. I wore a beautiful blue suit—skirt, blouse, and jacket—and a crown of flowers, with an attached veil over my hair and face. There may have been all of 12 people there, but in that group were two pastors.

L. W. Taylor officiated at the wedding. Pastor Andre Rochat took our photos and his wife, Joyce, came with him. I was so very happy and excited as I walked into the Cheeseman's home. They had decorated it beautifully. The entry seemed filled with flowers, and the staircase was decorated with bells, ribbons, and streamers of my colors—pink, blue, and white. All the living room furniture had been removed, and it made a very lovely site for our wedding. In the dining room ribbons of pink, blue, and white crepe paper flowed from the chandelier to an old-fashioned long wooden table that was set with crystal. There, the wedding cake and gifts awaited us. Cynthia and Cyril were there. Cynthia played the "Wedding March" on the piano, and Cyril was Roger's best man. My mother and Cyril signed our marriage certificate.

Before the wedding began Mother and Ruth went upstairs with me and made sure that my cheeks were pinched pink and my veil hung just right. Roger wore a beautiful gray suit he had bought for $100. That was a lot of money in 1947! He'd won the money sometime before by betting on the horse races. Supernatural beings had told him which ones would win.

Roger had the most beautiful black, wavy hair. I remember when we started dating that he had his hair slicked back with some kind of oil. I could hardly wait to get my hands on his hair and give him a good shampoo. On our wedding day his hair was all I had wanted, so full and rich and wavy black. He was so handsome, tall, slim, and proud of me. What is really touching to me is that Roger said that we wanted only a small wedding. We had no money, but friends who were very well-off wanted to give us a large church wedding. Roger expressed our being touched with the care these members gave us, but told them, "It would be better for us to have just a small wedding."

Arthur and Ruth Cheeseman now lived with Art's father. He had invited them to share his humble home, now lonely and empty to him since his wife had died. Art and Ruth asked if we would consider being married in their home. We were so pleased to have a home wedding, small like Roger and I wanted, and so it was to be.

To the music of the "Wedding March," I came down the staircase that led to the living room where we would be married. When Roger met me at the foot of the stairs, he took the hand that had been injured at birth and wrapped it around his arm, so gently, and led me into the living room where the guests awaited our entrance. I was overwhelmed with happiness. I truly thought my heart might explode as it was beating so fast with joy. After Pastor Taylor had pronounced us man and wife, and said, "Roger, you may kiss the bride," I burst into tears. That so upset poor Roger. "Are you sorry?" he asked me.

"No . . . I am just soooo happy," I cried.

Such memories of love!

chapter 8

MAC AND CHEESE—
EVERYWHERE!

We left the Cheeseman's in a taxi to go to our home, and whenever we stopped at a traffic light people would tap the car or press their faces against the windows and call out in English or French such things as, "Congratulations!" or "We wish you happiness!" We giggled all the way, not knowing how those people knew we had just been married. Surely our friends attached something to the taxi, but Roger and I were oblivious to nearly everything but each other.

Our marriage began with skimpy belongings. We were very poor, but so much in love. We had just a small bedroom and a living room. Entering our first home after the wedding, we saw a vase of roses and a card wishing us happiness that our landlords had placed there. It was truly a humble way to live. The owners passed through our living room to enter and exit, as we did also. We were grateful we had a door on our bedroom.

After a few weeks, our landlady informed us that we needed to take our baths together as we were using too much water. Roger and I looked at each other and said, "OK." It was even fun. What was really nice about living in our small apartment was how close it was to where Roger worked. Roger embroidered bridal gowns and women's evening wear at a nearby factory. Our first furni-

43

ture was a card table, folding chairs, and a bookcase with a glass door where we kept our treasures—the Bible and some Ellen G. White books. The French Mission had only about 30 members and that was where we worshipped. They gave us the *Conflict of the Ages* series for a wedding gift. We both loved the books. However, Roger loved them a little more than I did. During the first weeks of our marriage, wherever we were, on streetcars especially, Roger sat reading and reading and reading. I'd say to him, "Some day you'll be sorry. Here I am sitting beside you, a new wife, and you don't talk with me."

Roger would set his book down and put his arm around me. "I'm sorry," he'd apologize. "I love you." But soon I decided I'd better start bringing something to read, too, and that is how our marriage went. He was reading, and I was learning to read a lot. I later got involved in making things for our babies, so knitted and crocheted on many a trip.

Roger's thirst for knowledge of God was unquenchable. He just could not get enough of the Bible and the information that God had inspired Ellen White to write for the world to read. Roger's life was so directed toward the Lord that sharing about Jesus was his whole life. At that time he was working at a Jewish embroidery factory and pulling in a steady, good wage. That was where Roger had met Cyril who gave him Bible studies. Since Roger was reading so much of the Word, we wondered if an accident at the factory was not a trap of an evil angel. A needle broke in the machine, and a part of the needle flew up and wedged in his right eye. He was rushed to the hospital where he received help. We believed that God truly intervened so that he did not have a permanent injury to his eyesight.

In December, just before Christmas, Roger's father paid us a visit. This was my first meeting with any of Roger's family. Dad Morneau had managed to haul a very large box up the staircase and set it down in our small living room. That staircase was not easy to navigate as it twisted and turned. I remember how Roger carried me up the stairs and over the threshold of our first home. Oh, how he puffed to get me all the way up! I was laughing, and he was laughing. Now sitting at our little table, we opened Dad Morneau's box. It was filled with gifts from all of Roger's brothers and sisters. There were Hudson Bay blankets of 100 percent wool (we Canadians treasure Hudson Bay blankets), green with black stripes, and sheets and pillow cases—oh, what a happy time we spent with Dad Morneau. Tears were shed as we talked about our faith, and I recall as with tears in his eyes, he said, "As long as we believe in the same God, we will make out alright."

Roger's father was very industrious. He was still traveling to Montreal, bringing in produce from New Brunswick. He brought lobsters and other shellfish, the things we know are unclean. Roger was blessed to have such a loving family.

Roger's mother died when he was 12 years old. The last thing that his mother talked about was that she hoped he would become a priest. When Roger had been very ill as a child, his mother dedicated him to the priesthood. His uncle was a bishop, and they were sure God had spared Roger's life so he could become a priest. "Always be grateful to others, Roger, for what others do for you," were his mother's remembered words. Roger was always very appreciative for whatever others did for him.

With the eye injury, for a while Roger could not leave home to work and that gave us time to think about moving. We'd lived in the upstairs apartment just a few months when Roger came to the decision that it would be better for us to find a place where we'd have more privacy. It seemed that the owners of our apartment were upset over the literature we'd been reading and had left on the table. So Roger found a really nice apartment on St. Hubert Street, Montreal. In fact, the only thing we didn't have in that apartment was an oven. But on the same floor was a kitchenette with a refrigerator, a range, and an oven for the use of all the residents in the building. I used that oven for many meals.

But sad to say, though my mother was a wonderful cook I had no skills in cooking. She'd always said to me, "You will have plenty of time to do these things when you're married." Well, now I was married—and I still didn't know how to cook.

Then Roger brought home a turnip for us to eat, for both of us loved mashed turnips. I picked it up and looked at it and I saw that it had a glazed surface like wax. I didn't know what to do, so I called my mother. "How do I cook this turnip?" I asked her. "It seems to be covered in clear wax."

"Why Hilda, don't you realize that you have to peel a turnip?" she laughed. "Then you wash it, cut it up in pieces, add a little water, and cook it. When it's done, mash it and add butter and salt for flavor."

That seemed easy enough, but Mom wasn't through. "You need to get a cookbook and learn how to cook," she told me. "How do you think the rest of us learned how to cook? We used a cookbook!"

I guess it was about time I learned to cook for it was during this time that I learned I was going to have our first baby, Donald. So I got a cookbook, and that turnip was ever so delicious. Then I learned how to make macaroni and cheese and potatoes with onions and cheese on top. The first time I made macaroni and cheese, I told Roger to go to the kitchenette and get our dinner out of the oven. I don't know what happened, but as he entered our apartment with the hot dish, he slipped! He didn't fall but all of a sudden, as he slipped, the casserole flew into the air, flipped, and landed on the floor upside down. Macaroni and cheese flew all over the apartment splattering the three windows and their Venetian blinds with onions, macaroni, cheese, and tomatoes. For months we washed that dinner off of walls, ceiling, blinds, and windows. Oh, how many times we laughed over that!

Chapter 9

DEPENDING
ON THE LORD

One Sunday Roger and I were tidying up the apartment when we heard a knock at our door. Roger opened the door and saw a gentleman we had never met. He had heard about Roger and me through the church we attended, the French Mission in Montreal. The Mission had employed a young man and his wife, John Williams, and John had a lot to do with the Adventist publishing house. He had told R. J. Campbell about us, and now Pastor Campbell was at our door. He introduced himself and asked if he could spend a few minutes talking with us as he thought we would be interested in what he had to tell us. And that was Roger's introduction to the Adventist colporteur work.

We were both young in the church. I had canvassed one summer but Roger had no awareness of even what it was. Pastor Campbell left some informational material for Roger to read, and asked us to pray about it for the French-speaking people really needed someone who spoke French to get our published books into their community. Dear Pastor Campbell didn't apply any pressure. He just said he would get back to Roger. Roger and I prayed earnestly about it. He felt that God wanted him to do this for, as he said, it was a real calling to work for the French Catholics, many who had little understanding of the love of Jesus that the Word of God would reveal.

Some of the books Roger sold were on how to live healthfully. The health message was also important for Roger to share. You will need to understand that Roger had a weakness in that he literally could not be around sick people. It truly made him sick! If they vomited, he vomited; if they were in pain, he was in pain. It was God only who helped Roger deal with many situations he encountered and to be able to help with natural remedies. I remember a dear little family who lived right next door to us. They had six or more children, and the baby, about 8 months old, was having convulsions. Of course they were terribly frightened. Roger went over to help and prayed, reading from one of the books he sold on good health. Then he placed cold compresses on the forehead of the convulsing baby. Almost immediately the baby responded and became calm.

Because I was a nurse, Roger would rather I had gone to help them instead of he, but I was caring for our own baby at that time. But God truly used Roger, in that situation and in many more where people needed hands-on, practical help.

Roger started working as a colporteur in Montreal, walking up and down those high, steep stairways. A lot of those homes were at three and four stories, and the stairs were on the outside of the buildings. The Lord blessed Roger with sales and contacts. The colporteur work made us aware of how much we depended upon the Lord to provide for our daily needs.

I had had to leave my nursing work when I was about six months along with our first baby, and that meant that Roger's work had to bring in all the money we would need as a growing family. But we never had trouble making ends meet. We never lived in luxury, but the Lord always provided our needs and then some—with strong health, good attitudes, and happy hearts. Our future always looked bright and beautiful, perhaps because Roger always was an up-person. I never saw him depressed. Not ever. He believed in the Lord—His care and His promises, memorizing large portions of Scripture and the Spirit of Prophecy to encourage him, and me—that God was always there and would take care of His children.

chapter 10

THE MONSIGNEUR'S PHOTO

It was in January 1948, that Roger went into the colporteur work—selling Seventh-day Adventist books door-to-door. We were living in Montreal. Some of the church members of the St. Lawrence French Mission and also Roger were canvassing there. Toward the end of the year we learned that colporteur leaders were holding a recruiting and training program in Toronto. Roger was interested in going. But before it began, Pastor Doreau asked Roger and me if we would be willing to move to St. Rose, a small French town outside of Montreal. We were needed to assist a certain family whose adult son had not been faithful in going to church yet had asked the French Mission pastor in Montreal for help. His mother was bedridden and needed assistance.

Pastor Doreau made arrangements with the family to give us free living expenses while taking care of the son's mother. We had our own entrance, kitchen, bathroom, and bedroom with a private door to the main house. Should they need help, they would be able to call upon us easily by coming to the door between our living quarters.

So we moved from Montreal to St. Rose just before Christmas. Donald, our firstborn, was almost 3 months old. Roger had committed himself to attend the Colporteur Institute, so he left for Toronto soon after we moved. It was the day before New Year's, 1949, and the training session would last a week. What a long time that was for me to be alone with our baby. It was my first separation from Roger, and here I was in a strange town, in a house with people I didn't know, and our boxes had not been unpacked. We did not even have a telephone.

The days dragged by, but at last Roger returned. Now our lives were filled with happiness and great faith in what God had for our future.

Not too many months went by before the dear Christian lady I cared for went to sleep in her Savior. Her son, who was around 30 years old, had a girlfriend who was in her 20s, like myself, and I was the one who broke the news of the mother's passing to her.

It was morning. Roger was out canvassing and the elderly woman's son was at work. When I told this young woman that her boyfriend's mother had just died, she was terrified. She screamed and cried hysterically. It frightened me so! I tried to comfort her. I tried to assure her that God was in control and told her the little I knew that his mother was not a spirit and not running around the house as a spirit.

But she was so frightened and distraught that I was concerned she was going to go into a kind of a fit which I was in no condition to handle. I prayed and prayed. Her background was Catholic, and I am sure that was why she was so misinformed about death. I understood, as I, too, had been Catholic.

It may have been a few weeks later that Roger was away canvassing the day Donald developed pneumonia and had serious trouble breathing. I did everything I could think of to comfort him and help him get better, but it was a difficult time. The doctor came to the house and told me to place Donald under a tent with a vaporizer near his bed. When Roger came home, we both stayed up with Donald that night and through many other long nights until he was well again.

When we left St. Rose after the woman's death, Roger continued to colporteur in Montreal as well as around the small towns and cities like St. Hyacinth and St. John. At this time we lived in St. Jerome, in a second-floor apartment. I didn't work then, but stayed at home to care for Donald who was around 1 year old, just walking. The apartment had a room for Donald where my mother, Annie, also slept when she was visiting. Roger and I made the living room into our bedroom. We reached the apartment by a staircase outside the building, and the outside door entered into our kitchen.

It was here that Roger and I had a harrowing experience. The Catholic priest announced in St. Jerome that a man was going around town selling religious literature. The priest said that no one should buy this literature nor have anything to do with the salesman, as he was trying to get them to leave the Catholic Church.

A few weeks had gone by since we'd heard this, then this unbelievable experience happened. About midnight there was a knock at the kitchen door, the outside door. Of course, we and our son were asleep. Roger got up and answered the door. Two policemen, big men, filled the doorway. They told Roger that they had come to inspect our apartment because they had heard that he was distributing literature that was not appropriate. So they walked through the bedroom where Donald was sleeping and then into our bedroom at the front of the house.

Sitting up in bed, the covers clutched to my chest, I was terrified to see these two policemen stride in. But there on our dresser—so remarkable—Roger had placed a picture of his uncle who was the archbishop in the

Province of New Brunswick. This uncle had just been or-
dained as an archbishop of the Catholic Church. One of
the policemen said, "Look! That's a picture of the
'Monsigneur'! What are we doing here? These are good
people. What are we doing here?"

They quickly excused themselves and left. We had
been so terrified. We got on our knees and just cried and
thanked God for His help. We realized how Satan was
working and how God had protected us. During the re-
maining time we were in St. Jerome, Roger never had any
more trouble with the priests.

Downstairs from our apartment lived a family that had
a few children. The older girl, Madelaine Dubey, was a
beautiful girl of 17 or 18. She had numerous questions
about religion so Roger was giving her Bible studies. We'd
lived there not quite a year when Madelaine fell in love
with Jesus and His Word, and wanted to be baptized. She
had never been to our church, so Roger and I took her
one Sabbath. We didn't have a car—Roger used a bicycle
for transportation with his work—so we took a bus to
church. Roger had talked to the pastor at St. Lawrence
Mission about Madelaine so you can imagine our confu-
sion and distress when the pastor repeatedly avoided both
her and us that Sabbath. He literally turned his back on us.
Roger and I were heartbroken.

Then when we returned home we found that
Madelaine's mother had discovered her daughter had gone
to church with us and she was very angry. These factors
influenced our move back to Montreal. The other reason
was that I became pregnant again, this time with our
daughter, and needed medical help. The experience of
such coldness from our pastor toward Madelaine was dev-
astating and took years for us to breathe easily about it.

chapter 11

TWO WHEELS
FOR FOUR

When Roger finished working Montreal and the surrounding smaller towns, we moved where he could work for the people in Saint-Hyacinth. Our children were young—Linda was just 2 months old and Donald was 2 years. We lived in a two-story house that had an apartment above and one below. We had the apartment below.

Roger was so willing to make ends meet that when he and our family had needs, he set out to do some very creative things. The couple above us had a small baby, so one of their mothers was living with them. That grandmother and her husband had once owned a tailoring shop in Montreal. Roger needed a new suit, and decided he was going to attempt to sew one for himself. He found the material he needed, got his instructions, and started making the suit. But some of the instructions were confusing. Despite everything, he could not understand them at all. So this dear grandmother came down and helped Roger lay out the pattern and explained the instructions to him. Within about two months Roger had a lovely suit. (He'd had a handsome suit when we got married but that was some years before, and it showed wear and tear.)

Though Roger worked with few resources, he showed so much trust in God that he never complained. I had been a little worried for I'd often seen a car parked in our driveway while Roger was away, and the people stayed in the car. I wondered who they were and why they were there. Because there was such animosity from the Catholic priest toward Roger's work, I was very concerned and prayed often for Roger to come home soon. I had much concern for our safety.

But our lives were going to change. Dear Brother Brusy from the Bible Publishing House, the King's Way, in Oshawa, Ontario, came to visit Roger in regard to his house-to-house sales work. Roger's only means of transportation for himself and the books he carried with him was a bicycle, one I had been given from my parents. So not only was it old, it was a girl's bike, too! The last thing that Pastor Brusy said to Roger was, "I am going back to the Ontario and Quebec Conference and tell them that we cannot permit a canvasser going from door-to-door on a bicycle. We need to do something to get him a better means of transportation."

Not too many weeks went by before the conference arranged for Roger to have a small Prefect, a used 1950, Canadian distributed British Ford. It was a two-passenger car, but it had room enough in the back for two little children. Just room enough! We'd been taking the bus to get to church every Sabbath. It was not easy, but we were young and glad to do it. But when the dark blue Prefect was brought to the house, we were filled with joy. You cannot know how happy we were.

During this time Roger had a deep desire to go back home to New Brunswick, and having a car now made it possible. It was at least 200 miles away and we could never have made the trip without it. It was wonderful for us to take the children, now age 4 and 2, to visit the rest of Roger's family. I'd never met them. Roger hadn't seen his family for a long time, and oh, how they loved the children, Roger, and me. They were so warm and welcoming. So friendly! Roger had brought Christian slides and tapes with us, for he hoped he could share his faith and new understanding of the Bible with his family.

In the evenings all the families would join us in the large living room as Roger shared his love of God. Back then his family did not speak English, so Roger and I shared fluently in French—a true gift for me as I was never that comfortable with French. They were overjoyed each night, and at the end of the slides, tapes, or whatever he was showing, they would say, "When are you showing the next movie?" This brought such joy to Roger.

There would be 20 or so people in the living room, children and adults. Many times Roger had to stop what he was showing to explain what they were seeing and to answer questions. They could not understand why they did not know these things as they had a bishop in the family. Why didn't he bring them this information?

Despite the many trips we made to visit Roger's family, his uncle, the bishop, was never able to come to be with us. We never quite understood how that could be. Yet he, as the local bishop, may have known it would have caused a conflict. Certainly our God would have known and kept us from disharmony in the family. This dear Catholic family won our hearts for their sincerity and acceptance of the teachings they were hearing. They thought it just too good to be true, for they were learning things they had never heard before. We saw no visible changes of lifestyle for Roger's family, yet we knew that God's Word was enlightening, and in heaven we would see its result.

chapter 12

MOVING ON

After Roger had worked Saint-Hyacinthe quite thoroughly, we moved down further southeast of Quebec Province so that Roger would be able to do his canvassing work in those small towns. We were in Virgil, a little town on the border of Ontario, maybe 15 miles from New York. Another colporteur joined us, living about 20 miles from us. While we were in Virgil we were afflicted with hay fever. For some reason, there Roger started having hay fever symptoms like I'd been having. When we went to Brunswick, we were better. At Virgil, our eyes and nose ran terribly and our ears were blocked. We discovered that when we were in New Brunswick, our nose and eyes stopped itching. If we went back to Virgil when the pollen was around, we would again become ill.

One time that sticks out in my mind was the day Roger and I awoke very early in the morning. Our heads were all stuffed up and it was hard to breathe. By then Linda was potty trained, but we still had lint-free courtesy diapers that she no longer needed. There we were, sitting on the edge of the bed, using the diapers as napkins, sneezing our heads off. We both completely drenched the diapers. Roger looked at me and said, "Let's just go home. We're going back to where we can breathe." Roger's folks were overjoyed to have us back in Edmonston, New Brunswick, where Roger grew up.

His brother, Adolph, was out of work, so he said to Roger, "Why don't we go down to Niagara Falls and look for jobs? It's been a few months since I've worked here."

"Will it be alright if I leave you here and go with my brother and look for a job?" Roger asked me. Of course I said yes. I was glad he had an opportunity to find work. They were away three weeks.

Roger told me that he needed to get out of the colporteur work because of an ongoing problem with the Book and Bible House. No doubt, looking back, God had other plans for us than colporteuring. While in Niagara Falls, Ontario, Roger had found a man who had built a new duplex. It was at Niagara-on-the-Lake, a place at the southern part of Ontario. Once home, Roger turned to me and said, "Honey, I asked the owner if he would rent to us? Would you mind?"

I never minded what Roger thought was right. "No, honey, whatever you think," I assured him. So we came down to Niagara-on-the-Lake.

There Roger got a job selling cemetery lots. All of this packing and moving away from the Montreal area took place around our 1953 wedding anniversary. The night before the move, we had everything ready to go when some acquaintances from church came over and invited us to join them in viewing the coronation of Queen Elizabeth II on television. TV was still a novelty in those years, and we were so excited to see such a sight.

So we made the move. Linda was 3 and Donald was 5. Quite a distance from the house we moved into was a pond, and we stressed to both children that they must *never* go down there. Yet, right after we moved in, my little ones found the pond. The first I knew it was when Donald ran to me, yelling, "Mama! Mama! Linda's in the pond!"

I flew out the door and ran full speed, yelling at the pastor who was working in the garden next door, "Help me! Help me! My little girl is in the pond. My little darling . . . please help!"

All the time I yelled, I was running. That precious man, that pastor, brought his rake with him and ran with me. We got there and saw Linda floating face down a ways from the shore, her little dress spread out across the water. The pastor stretched out flat on the bank and reached with his rake to catch her and pull her to shore. We got her up on the bank but she was lifeless and limp. I was terrified, but we worked with her until she revived. He used artificial resuscitation—turning her over, getting the water out of her lungs, then breathing into her until she coughed on her own. At last we thought it safe to move her, and he carried her to the house. I watched Linda all afternoon and all night long. She slept and slept.

From that day on, Linda was terrified of water. I couldn't wash her hair without her screaming so loud the whole neighborhood would hear her. Only when she grew to an adult was God able to heal her of that fear. Today, Linda loves her swimming pool.

Thinking of it today, it is a memory of a dreadful, terrible time when God truly saved my daughter. God knew that the pastor was in the garden. God knew he would bring the rake and run with me and know how to revive a drowning child. How much this shows the care of our God for His children.

ABOVE: The Mousseau family.
Back row (left to right):
Raphael (my father), John, Edna,
Ories, Flowe, Milton, Edwidge,
Salem, Rubina.
Front row: Grandpa (Euchere)
and Grandma (Mary) Mousseau.

LEFT: Roger's parents,
Freddy and Clairida, when they
were married in June 1914.

These photos were taken while I was studying to become a licensed practical nurse.

Cyril and Cynthia
Grosse with Cyril, Jr.

Roger at Cyril's for his first Bible study. Demonic worship was part of Roger's young adult life until his conversion to Jesus.

Photos of Roger and me taken on our first date.

Our wedding day,
September 20, 1947,
at the home of
Arthur and Ruth
Cheeseman,
Montreal, Canada.

LEFT: Roger's uncle, archbishop in the province of New Brunswick for the Roman Catholic Church.

BELOW: Our young family—Donald is 4 years old and Linda is 2 years old in this photo.

BELOW: The Morneau men (left to right): Roger, Edgar, Freddy (Dad), Edmond.

ABOVE: At home with the children in Buffalo, New York.

LEFT: Linda mothering our third child, Daniel, in 1963.

Donald and Linda returning from gathering eggs at our home in Curriers, New York.

LEFT: On the go . . .

BELOW: Roger's success as a salesman—praise God!

RIGHT AND BELOW:
Dan and Karen Houghton
interview Roger for Hart Research.
You'll notice Krystal snuggled
close to Roger in both pictures!

Happy times—
Roger and Mother

GOD'S MIRACLE COPIER

THIS COPIER RAN OUT OF TONER
ON MARCH 10TH, 1993. IT IS NOW
RUNNING ON A PRAYER, PRODUCING
BEAUTIFUL HIGH QUALITY COPIES.

GLORY TO GOD IN THE HIGHEST!

Roger's "miracle" copier. He made a plaque that remained above the copier to honor God for His gift of ink during 22 months of constant use *after* the toner ran out.

One of Roger's prayer towers.

Any humble place can be a prayer altar—this was Roger's favorite.

RIGHT: Sharing a meal with Norman and Florence Doss.

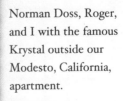

Norman Doss, Roger, and I with the famous Krystal outside our Modesto, California, apartment.

Doug Batchelor invited Roger to the Sacramento Central Seventh-day Adventist Church for a question and-answer session.

Roger and Doug with a stack of prayer requests before them. These two men were sharing their personal experiences of answered prayer. God will work with anyone and everyone, faulty people like Roger and me, who come to know God and who then want to be like Him. Prayers are answered when people believe Him, trust His promises, and strive to follow Him. Then ask whatever you will and experience His power in the answers He gives.

Roger and I.

Grace Villeneuve and I met by a divine appointment at the General Conference session in Toronto, Canada, in 2000. Grace shared her faith with me in Montreal as a young woman.

My dear friend Marjorie Kraft Stirling and I outside our apartments at Napa Valley Adventist Retirement Estates, Yountville, California.

Our older son,
Donald.

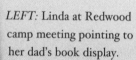

LEFT: Linda at Redwood
camp meeting pointing to
her dad's book display.

Our younger son, Daniel,
and his wife, Cheryl.

chapter 13

THE YEARS SLIP BY

That winter Roger sold cemetery lots for a couple of months. It was a strange winter for it had never happened before—pansies blooming right before Christmas. They pushed their sweet way through a thin layer of snow. The area where we'd moved was the fruit belt of Ontario, and that was a year for the records. I'm not sure if God did that to make our lives happy, but its warmth and the lovely pansies thrilled our hearts.

During different times of our marriage, Mother lived with us. So this year, around the Christmas holidays, Mother came from Montreal and stayed at Niagara-on-the-Lake. Roger was working to get passports for the three of us, and on our passport applications he checked the box indicating we would want to become U.S. citizens. The papers came, and the process was begun.

Everything Roger put his hand or mind to do, he did well. He learned how to sell cemetery lots by memorizing 20 pages of reasons why people should purchase one or more. Roger sold a number of lots, but he did not think this was God's plan for him. "I know we are being blessed by it," Roger told his boss. "But I am just not comfortable when I know Jesus is coming soon." They were sorry to see him go as he did well in selling for them.

When Roger stopped selling cemetery lots, he no

longer had a job. But as we discussed what we should do next, we were aware of the needs of our growing family. Donald was 5 and would be in school the next year, so we made the decision to move to the States. The children were beginning to grow up, needing education, and we wanted only Christian education for them. Roger suggested there would be an advantage if we moved to a place where Adventist schools were established, so in 1954 we moved to Niagara Falls, New York.

Roger's first job was selling Electrolux vacuum cleaners door-to-door. In those times, making ends meet was not easy. Mother helped us in those days. Our problems were not only financial. We were having trouble breathing again, partly because of the chemical produced by the factories in Niagara Falls. Then while working with the vacuum cleaners, Roger met Mr. Goodrich who owned the store that sold aluminum windows and doors—that was when they first came out. We moved to Buffalo, New York, where Mr. Goodrich's company was located and Roger later worked there. It also would be where Donald would begin his education at the Adventist grade school.

It was good that Roger was settled in a job, yet we knew I needed to help with the finances. I was a nurse, trained in Canada, and my degree was not recognized in the States. Then I was made aware of a possible way to get my license quickly. The Board of Education was willing to train nurses at Children's Hospital in Buffalo, and the government would fully pay for my education. All they required of those selected for this program was that they would work for a year in one of the three Buffalo hospitals. There were 200 applicants for this training, but only 28 would be chosen. I was one of the 28, and passed my

State Board exam a year later. How grateful we felt for these God-given favors.

I look back now and recall that one of Roger's close friends, a public school principal, wrote a very kind reference letter to the Board for me. That must have been a way that the Lord moved to help them choose me. When I had my license, I worked nights so Roger could be home with the children. I was committed to finishing the course and to give the year's work for Children's Hospital. Years later, my brother-in-law, Roger's sister's husband, told us that my name was on a list of former hospital employees from those years I worked at the Children's Hospital in Buffalo so long ago. I felt it was an honor as I loved the work there.

Mother usually gave care to the elderly in their homes, living in with them. When we moved from Niagara Falls, New York, to Buffalo, New York, Mother found work again. I don't recall whether she saw an ad in the Buffalo newspaper or if it was through a mutual friend, but she found employment with a retired Buffalo judge who requested assistance in his home because of a disability that confined him to a wheelchair. This position required her to live in the house, giving Judge Chipman care as needed. She worked with him for two or three years.

During the end of the time Mother worked for Judge Chipman my father contacted her and asked her to come back to him where he lived in Beaupré, Canada. It was a big decision, but Mother decided to do it, giving up her application to be a United States citizen because she felt certain that life with Dad would work out. So she moved back to him.

In about 1955, maybe eight years after his baptism, Roger was asked to give a sermon at the Batavia, New

York, Seventh-day Adventist Church. At that time Roger and I were still young parents, and the church nominating committees repeatedly chose Roger for responsible positions such as church elder and adult Sabbath school teacher. He gladly accepted anything that he could do to further the work of God, and took these opportunities with appreciation and diligence to see that they were done well. I don't recall when or where it was that Roger was first asked to take the Sabbath sermon, but he was often asked to do so when a pastor had to be away. That may have been the case in Batavia. In the congregation that day was the author June Strong. She met us after the service and invited our family over for Sabbath lunch. This was no small feat to host parents and two children, for Linda and Donald, were about 5 and 7 years old. We had a delightful lunch and visit, and the friendship between our families began.

When we first settled in Buffalo, Donald was beginning to ride a bicycle and I worried about him all the time as he was riding out in the city streets. Later when Mother left us to go back with Dad (so we no longer had her help), and the children were not learning reading and writing skills at our church school, we found ourselves in a difficult time that needed an important decision. On a special Sabbath afternoon after church we were all resting on the big bed—Roger, Linda, Donald, and me. The children told Roger, "It would be so nice to live in the country, Daddy, like the Richards live." Mr. and Mrs. Richards belonged to the church we attended in Buffalo, and on a few Sabbaths they'd invited us over for lunch and to spend the Sabbath hours with them. They lived about 30 miles east of Buffalo.

It was such a joy to go to their home. They treated us as if we were their children. Mr. Richards told stories about the Sabbath and the many experiences of the pioneers in the Adventist faith. It just warmed our hearts with the expressive ways Mr. Richards spoke of the Lord. They had a huge barn with two big doors that opened out. In the barn was a swing that hung down from the rafters where two people could sit on the wide board. We'd push the children way out and they just loved it, as Roger and I did too. The Richards had a pond out in the woods where they enjoyed walking before sunset. He would take a long stick and tickle the bellies of the frogs that held still for his massages. Let me tell you, it was such a peaceful and lovely time as we sang and together closed Sabbath.

I remember one time when the Richards were going to visit their son in Loma Linda, California. They invited us to their home, and said, "We're going to California for a month, and want you to come and visit the farm any time you like." And we did. We so appreciated them and their farm.

At first when Roger heard that the children and I wanted to live in the country, he resisted. He said, "How can I travel so far into Buffalo? It is just too far to get to work from the country."

The children said, "Oh, Daddy, please, *please!*"

I tried to keep quiet. I didn't want to try to pressure him. Then I remember Roger turning to me and saying, "How can I say no, when all three of your hearts are set on the country? Let's go out to the Richards and see if they know of any house to rent."

Roger may not have realized he was following God, and thought he was just pacifying the family but at least he was willing to look into it. When we got to the Richards, they said, "Surely, there must be a place around here for rent. Let's go look."

We prayed together before we left, asking God to help us find a place if He wanted it for us. Mr. Richards drove us around in Curriers and Holland where they lived. Eventually we drove by a farmhouse with a dairy and chicken farm. There were lots of cows in the pasture. As we passed the main farmhouse, we saw another house, set back a ways. The house had its own driveway and it looked like no one lived there. Driving on its road, we could see the pasture with the cows and that the house was indeed empty. Nearby was a long, narrow building that we later learned held rows and rows of laying hens. Mr. Richards said, "Let's go back and talk to the owner, Mr. Miller."

We retraced our path and got to the Miller's house, reaching them as they were just getting out of their car. Mr. Richards said, "We are wondering if you'd like to rent your house over there. We noticed it was empty."

Mr. Miller answered right away, "No. It's not for rent. I'm keeping it for a hired man."

We felt bad about it and showed it, but Mr. Richards was friendly and thanked him for understanding our disappointment. He turned around, got into the car, and started backing out of the driveway. Then Mr. Miller ran after us. "Would you like to see the house?" he called.

We were thrilled, and we all went over to see it together. It had two huge windows that looked out into the pasture. I could see the Miller's home from it as well. Underneath the window sill were the most beautiful flowers—hollyhocks, and delphiniums. Hummingbirds flitted around the flowers, making it a most welcoming sight. The men talked, and Mr. Miller gave Roger the OK to rent it. This was 1961.

Mr. Miller was a quiet, soft-spoken man, easy to get

along with. And his wife, Mary, became like a mother to me. She was talkative and so friendly. We loved living there.

The Millers knew a lot about Adventists and once, some years later, Mr. Miller invited Roger to speak at his Sunday-keeping church. Mary Miller had told me that there were many Adventist books in the attic of one of the houses they owned. We had agreed to share a day and go see them, but it never happened. I am sure that over the years we became to them as their family, as they came to be ours. We shared the birth of our youngest child, Daniel, in 1963, and they shared Sunday meals and their son's graduation and birthdays. Indeed, we loved them.

We met Glen Coon and his dear wife at a weekend retreat in South Stoukely, New York, and were overwhelmed with this man's energy and his radiance with the love of Jesus. How he loved to have the congregation sing his trademark song with all their hearts as he led them with his precious booming voice: "Come and go with me, to my Father's house . . ." How people loved his genuine, loving "Coon hug."

Glen had suffered with bouts of depression, but learned to pull himself through them by praising God for all the simple things in life. "Thank You for the door, the sunshine, the birds, the grass . . ." He told us how all his troubles rolled away through the praise sessions. How many books he wrote that encouraged us and thousands of others!

Because of his last name, Coon, I found cards with raccoons and mailed them to Glen and his wife with love. Roger and I often said that we would like to be like them. They were a tremendous blessing to the church. His wife had the most delightful laugh and they made a wonderful team. We counted it joy that we had them as our friends.

When Daniel was born Mother came to help me with the other children. She was such a blessing. Afterward, Mother returned to her home in Beaupré. Dad, however, was getting paranoid, drinking a lot, and at times even threatened her life. He had a gun, and Mother was very concerned about the gun. I didn't know any of this until I got a call from one of my father's coworkers at the paper mill. He told me that things were not going well for Mother, as Dad was out of control and irrational, even at work. This coworker was concerned about Mother still being with my dad. He said that I should try to get her to come back to live with us.

So arrangements were made for us to meet her at the train in Niagara Falls, Ontario. She was coming home. All three of us cried when we were together again. After being with Dad for four years she had grown so thin and frail. All she had when she arrived back with us was a small trunk. In it were her only worldly possessions. What is remarkable is that all through our lives, Mother could make two cents out of one. Consequently, many a time she had helped Roger and me through difficulties. Now, it was our time to help her.

Mother and Roger loved each other. She was his mother, too. I could hear them talking in the kitchen at nights. When I'd come home from work I'd find them laughing and having such a good time together. It was a joy to see them. Mother was such a blessing to me as the children were busy little ones, and Daniel was still a baby. But it wasn't too long before she knew her life was not over, and she started thinking of going back to work.

When she got a small car and made friends with the gas station owners, they asked her if she would take care of their mother. So she did. No longer accepting live-in jobs, Mother drove from our home. After her patient died, she got acquainted with an attorney who wanted her to care for someone in his family. She worked with him for many months.

Mother had some negative feelings about our faith, so we knew she would not enjoy the trip we were planning. Camp meeting was coming up in New York at the end of June, and Mother did not want to go. I told her, "Mom, you have friends in Niagara Falls, Ontario. Why don't you go across to be with some of them while we're gone?"

So she did. And while we were at camp meeting, Mother found a place to live there at a senior citizens' residence that was operated by the government of Ontario. She lived there quite a while, eight to 10 years.

chapter 14

SCARY TIMES, HAPPY TIMES

I was working at a hospital in Springville, New York, about 22 miles from Curriers, and Donald truly put me, both as a mother and a nurse, through many a difficult time. Somehow he seemed prone to accidents and when he was 13, he was in a serious accident. He was in the habit of riding his bike to the Millers after school to offer to help on the farm. While cycling home one dark, rainy evening, he was hit by a car.

I received the phone call at the first floor where I was on duty that night. It was someone from the ambulance team telling me that my son was on his way to the emergency room—just down the hall from where I was working. Someone came and covered for me, and I phoned our doctor, Dr. Meenan, who came and treated Donald's fractured lower right leg, setting it in a cast and sending him home with me. Roger must have been away working.

Then when he was 17, Donald jumped down from a tractor and dislocated his hip, a slipped epiphysis. The doctor said, "Hilda, we are going to have to send him to Buffalo, and you'll have to go with him in the ambulance."

Before we left, Dr. Meenan gave him a painkiller for the pain. He said, "If he starts getting pain, you will need to have this to get him through." Donald was admitted to

Children's Hospital for surgery, which he had the next morning. Afterward he said thankfully, "Mother, I have no more pain." It must have been excruciating. He was there a few days, and then discharged, and we went home.

After the surgery Donald was not able to attend school for a long time, so a dedicated Christian woman, one of the teachers from his school, came to the house during the school week to help him so he would not be delayed from graduating. Donald had only to hear his lessons to know them. He went through all his schooling with high grades. Donald was something like his father with memorization.

As all children do, Linda had her bouts with giving us concern, but one of the cutest scenes was when Roger, Linda, and I went out to gather the eggs from the henhouse near our home. Linda must have been about 11 years old. The eggs were in nests of hay, and each hen had its own little area. We would go in and search for the eggs. This day Linda went in and was standing on the hay, when her father called to her. "Linda, I don't want you to move," he said. "I want you to stay right there, honey. Be still."

Linda looked around as I did and saw what Roger saw: in the same nest where Linda stood a skunk was eating, probably an egg. Roger ran and got his camera and took a picture of Linda and the skunk. It is such a joy to have that memory recorded with a photo. The hens could come and go to their nesting cages. It was a good setup, and skunks had never been in the henhouse before. We're not sure how it found its way in, but there it was! We left the area quietly. When Roger went back later, the skunk was nowhere to be found. We still wonder how he found his way in and out.

A year or so later, we experienced a hurricane. It

passed through Curriers and tore most of the roof off of the Millers' church that was located at the Curriers' Crossroads, about a mile or so from where we lived. Linda, Danny, and I were very frightened. The sky was almost black and the winds howled. Linda ran and picked up Danny who'd been blown and caught at the fence. I was a short distance from them, and with difficulty we were able to reach the house with nature all out of control. It happened so quickly. The darkness, wind, and rain were so strong that it was horribly fearful. We fought to get to the house where we were safe. No injuries to people were recorded, but a lot of damage was done to buildings.

Roger continued to work for Mr. Goodrich and became one of the top salesmen. As an incentive, Mr. Goodrich offered cars and other awards to his salesmen. Roger won a car, and then another one! When he received the second car, he gave it to me. It was a good thing, as the car I was driving had been old to begin with and was ready to outright stop. It was a great help to have a new car.

One year Roger won an expensive entertainment center. Like most Americans at that time, I remember the day President Kennedy was shot and assassinated in 1963. Daniel was 4 months old. Roger had phoned me and told me to turn on the television as the President had been shot. We watched the news reports, and eventually the funeral and the long march to the cemetery, on the TV that was part of that entertainment center. That was a very dark time for all Americans as well as many across the world.

Mr. Goodrich had to revise his way of giving awards because Roger's winning two cars caused bad feelings among the other employees. Even so, we were so grateful to the Lord that He allowed us to have new cars just when we needed them so badly.

Roger's work was tough, because we lived out in the country and he had to travel far to find his customers. A friend of ours who worked for the telephone company lived near Syracuse, New York. He said, "You know, Roger, I would like to put in a word for you to my boss for your working for the phone company, selling ads for the yellow pages." That is how Roger went to work for the Leland Mast Telephone Company with their main office in Kansas and his office in Syracuse, New York.

chapter 15

GOD'S LIGHT
STILL SHINES

In 1969, we were living in Arcade when we moved to Hunt, New York, and began living in a motor home my father helped us purchase. At that time, through the invitation of Pastor A. J. Patzer, we were thinking of moving the motor home on to the property of the Letchworth church and considering it our home church. Shortly after this the annual week-long camp meeting was starting in upstate New York. Roger had earned respect from Pastor Patzer, the president of the New York Conference of Seventh-day Adventists, and he invited Roger to give his personal testimony at the camp meeting. I still have the letter he sent to Roger.

June 13, 1969

Dear Brother Morneau:

It was a distinct pleasure for us to have had the opportunity of being at Letchworth last Sabbath, June 7, and also to be in your home after the church service Sabbath afternoon.

I listened with a great deal of interest in regard to you accepting the Seventh Day Adventist faith and the number of Bible studies you had each evening which, of course, ultimately brought you into the Seventh Day Adventist Church.

Sabbath afternoon, July 5, at our camp meeting, we want to feature a number of soul winning phases of our work, and I would be delighted to have you on our program and for us to interview you in connection with the Sabbath afternoon program.

Would it be possible for you to be at our camp meeting Sabbath, July 5 . . .

Thank you so very much and looking forward to seeing you and with kindest Christian regards,

Yours in the Master's service,
A. J. Patzer, President

It was because of the comments of Elder Patzer and other dedicated friends of God that Roger knew the Lord was leading him to write his many stories of answered prayer.

Hunt, New York, is a small town near Nunda where I worked the night shift at Dansville Hospital. It was about seven miles to work, and the road took me over a couple of high hills. One night I left home around 10:30, needing to be on duty at 11:00. I'd almost reached the top of the first hill when suddenly my car would not go forward. I had no control over the steering, the brakes, or anything else. When I released my foot from the gas pedal, the car started rolling backward down the hill. I was terrified as the car naturally picked up speed as it descended the road. On the right side was an embankment, and on my left side was a deep trench with steep walls. Evenly spaced toward the edge of the trench, were steel rods to keep cars from going off the highway and into the trench.

I had no control over the car, and was helpless to do

anything but pray. "Oh, Lord, protect me from tipping over," I cried. The car swerved into the oncoming lane and then flew between the steel rods, not touching them, *bump, bump, bump* until it jolted to a violent stop at the bottom of the trench. My hands still grasped the steering wheel with all my might. I was amazed that I had no injury. First I thanked my Savior. Then I remembered that Roger, my loving husband, always kept a large flashlight in both of our cars. I found it and was so happy that it worked. I began waving the flashlight's bright beam high above me, toward the highway. The night was pitch dark but I could see light from the traveling vehicles above. I prayed, "Oh, Lord, You know that there is no way to get myself up this steep embankment." Shortly after that prayer, I heard a man's voice calling from the highway, "Are you all right?"

"I'm all right, but I can't get myself up the hill," I yelled. He walked down the embankment and helped me climb up with his support. This dear man drove me to Nunda where I could get to a phone. I called Roger and asked him to call the hospital, explaining that I would not be able to be on duty.

The story this dear man told me on the trip to Nunda could only have come from God. He lived in Warsaw, and had an evening job near Dansville. Something impressed him to go home a different way, a way that was much longer and even taking him the wrong direction, but he thought, *Why not!* So he was traveling down the highway to Nunda when he thought he saw a light shining at his right. The more he looked, the brighter the light. So he stopped his car and called out to me.

I never saw that man again and he didn't give me his name. Could he have been my guardian angel? Only in eternity will I know. But this I do know, I was in need of help, and God did answer my prayer.

After a year or so of Roger working for the company, they wanted to have him closer to the Syracuse office, and so they gave him a number of choices of where to move. He chose Binghamton, New York. Leland Mast gave credit to Roger for many of the successful ventures they experienced while he was with them. Roger became their sales manager. He had established Leland Mast among the French speaking people in Ste. John, New Brunswick, Canada, as well as other locations. Roger helped in settling and hiring the personnel for the branch office in Ste. John. He took us as a family with him whenever he could. It was good of the company to encourage Roger to take Daniel and me along. By that time our older children, Linda and Donald, were married.

Linda and her husband had two precious children, a son and a daughter. Roger and I so loved all our family, including the sons and daughters-in-law and especially our grandchildren. Then there had been some trouble that Linda and her husband could not work out, and her first marriage ended in divorce.

Linda was always bright. She went back to college and worked with legal offices as a secretary. Linda met her present husband, Mike Hatley, at Walla Walla College. His three children—Michelle, Christina, and James—from a previous marriage, lived with him. With Linda's two— Michael and Deborah—there were five children in the household. It gave both Roger and me a sense of well being that Linda and her children were settled. The joy of children is worth all the heartache in this life.

Our older son, Donald, went to college and became a registered nurse. We were so proud of his caring and nurturing profession and his many good choices, as I am still proud of him today. Donald has given us four grandchildren whom we dearly love—Danielle, Jennifer, Eden, and Delight. He has married more than once, and each of these dear wives has been as dear as our own children to Roger and me. Divorce is so very painful for all the family. One day we will have the pain behind us and rejoice that these families will be united under the banner of heaven.

Roger eventually left the phone company because of the pressure put on him to travel in the eastern states to get more business. For a short time after that, Roger worked with the Binghamton *Press*, the main newspaper in Binghamton, as an advertising salesman. He took pride in designing the ads for his customers, making everything from full-page ads to small ads, keeping abreast of the events in the community. This gave him many opportunities to make friends. He never had to work on Sabbath. His coworkers truly appreciated him, and Roger felt deeply for them as well, and was grateful to the *Press* for such a fulfilling job.

Then our pastor at Vestal Hills Seventh-day Adventist Church asked Roger if he would be willing to speak at the young people's meeting on a certain Friday night. Roger was an adult Sabbath school teacher and his class was well attended, but he did not know what he should talk about to the young people. When I got home from work the next morning Roger told me that he had wondered what to say, and had felt impressed to tell the group about his own experience with spiritualism. He had not talked about this for years and years. In fact, Roger had deliberately not spoken of it as he did not want our children to think of their father being involved with such darkness. But now our children were grown, out of our home, and on their own. His strong conviction to warn people of the dark spirit world is what prompted the whole story to unfold.

In that Friday night meeting was a visiting pastor, William R. Lawson, who worked with the blind and who was visiting family in the area. He was so impressed with the experiences Roger told that he approached him after the meeting and told him that his story needed to be put into print. Roger took him seriously, as a direction from God. It was then that he started handwriting the manuscript that later became *A Trip Into the Supernatural.*

Since leaving her area of New York, Roger and I had corresponded with the author June Strong. Now Roger contacted June for help in knowing what to do to prepare his story for publication. She was his mentor, guiding, suggesting, and referring him to the Review and Herald Publishing Association where one of the book editors, Gerald Wheeler, worked with him. The first manuscript Roger sent there was handwritten. It was sent back with a request for it to be typed, double spaced, to make it easier to read and evaluate. Roger had never typed, but he bought a manual typewriter and learned, pounding on the keys. Eventually he had his story typed and he sent it in again. It was accepted, and then the work between Gerald and Roger truly began. The published book came out in 1982.

After the successful response of readers to *A Trip Into the Supernatural,* people began to write to Roger. He read every letter and often sensitively wrote answers to their inquiries. Roger learned from these letters that many were desperately seeking God, but seemingly did not know how to have a personal, dynamic relationship with Him. Thinking about this, Roger determined to write about his personal experiences of prayer with and for his clients, showing what happened following his prayers. This he hoped would point his readers to talk with God and make Him their precious Friend, giving every concern to Him. So Roger began writing his first book on personal prayer. It was titled *Incredible Answers to Prayer*.

chapter 16

ROGER'S FIRST HEART ATTACK

December, 1984.

Mother had gotten rid of her car, so traveled by Greyhound bus to come visit us. She arrived in time for Thanksgiving and stayed with us until after the New Year holiday. We were living in Endecott, New York, at this time. One evening we drove Mother home to her apartment at the senior citizens' complex in Niagara Falls, Ontario, and stayed overnight. Roger slept in her bedroom and Mother and I slept together on the sofa in the living room.

Mother woke me up early that morning, saying, "Hilda, I don't know what's wrong with Roger. He was up and down all night."

I'd worked the night before we drove Mother back home, and had slept so deeply that I hadn't awakened to hear Roger moving around. When I went in to check on him, I could not believe my eyes. His color was ashen and he was perspiring profusely. Even so, he was going to attempt to take a shower. "No!" I told him. "We're going to the hospital right away." We got in the car to drive to the hospital back home in the States. I was driving, and immediately saw that Roger wouldn't make it that far. But I didn't know where the Niagara Falls, Ontario, hospital was. About a block from Mother's, I saw a pharmacy. I stopped, ran inside, and asked for directions, saying that my husband was seriously ill. God helped me get to the hospital.

I pulled up in front and ran into the emergency room, telling them that my husband was critically ill and to hurry and get him out of the car. They brought him in on a stretcher and disappeared behind closed doors. I sat in a waiting area until I could go into his room. I saw the ER physician run past me as I waited to be called to Roger. Later I learned that he was running to get the cardiac physician who was in the parking lot, on his way home. The two of them ran back to Roger. It seemed hours before I knew what was happening. Then the doctor came out and said they did not know if they could save him or not. They had rushed him into the ICU (Intensive Care Unit). This was in the Greater Niagara General Hospital.

While I sat near the ICU, two women sat nearby whose husbands were being cared for in there as well. One of the men had been in a car accident. The other woman's husband had a serious heart condition. Neither of them knew if their husbands would live. The wife of the car accident victim was very upset by her husband's condition and the realization that they had left all their belongings at a hotel in Niagara Falls, New York, where they were vacationing. I don't know how God gave me the strength, but I drove her to the hotel to get her things, and back to the hospital where we waited until we could finally see our husbands.

I had not yet called Mother to tell her what was happening. When I did, she was distant and uninterested. She didn't even come to the hospital to be with me. I felt so alone, as if I'd fallen into a deep, dark, black hole and was not able to come out. I remember being in the ER waiting room, just sitting there in shock. I do not remember whether I went to Mother's to sleep. She was so detached, saying things like, "If he does die, you'll have to go on." Those words gave me no strength or hope. Sometimes we do not understand why our own loved ones cannot be there for us, yet we know they themselves are going through such things that make it impossible for them to support us.

I thank God that He was there for Roger and me. Praise the Lord, within a week I was driving Roger back to Endecott and home. It was a true miracle, one that Roger wrote of in *Incredible Answers to Prayer*. I suppose that the things that Mother had gone through in her life had made her hardhearted, or somehow unable to be empathetic with me. It was so out of character for her to not be caring and loving. Certainly God was there for Roger and me—and for all the patients in the ICU at that time. As Roger's story tells, as critical as many of them were, they all lived.

By now Roger had retired from paid positions. He'd had one book written and published before he retired, *Trip Into the Supernatural*. His other books were written after his cardiomyopathy was diagnosed. This is what nearly took his life in the experience at Ontario Falls, Canada.

At home back in Endecott, Roger was recuperating from his heart episode, and most of his time was spent in bed. He was so weak and drained of energy that even coming downstairs for a meal wiped him out.

One day while shopping at the mall I passed their pet store. I stopped for a moment to look in the window and saw three Schnauzer puppies. They were so cute, I couldn't help myself. I went into the store and asked if I could hold one of them. As I held it I thought that maybe this would help Roger, giving him something that needed him. I called Daniel and told him "Meet me at the mall. I believe I've found something to help your dad feel better and to do well."

Twenty minutes later Daniel was at the pet store. He had the same trouble I did. All three puppies looked alike, and each was so cute. We couldn't decide which one was Roger's so we took the one in the middle. When we came home, of course Roger was in bed. Daniel held the puppy in his one hand and said, "Dad! Dad, look what I've got."

Roger looked up. "What's that for?"

"Dad, it's yours," Daniel said. "Mom bought a puppy for you."

"How can I take care of that? I can't even take care of myself."

He thought we'd gone crazy. Then Daniel put the puppy on Roger's bed, and it went right up to his face. Roger touched her soft fur and that was the beginning of a wonderful friendship between the two. They were inseparable.

Roger named her Krystal. She was beautiful—black with silver strands and areas of white through her wavy hair, making her very attractive. She had large dark eyes that melted our hearts, and such a happy disposition. Because Krystal needed to be taken outside now and then, Roger began to walk again. He eventually found that he needed different items to help him care for her, and that began the trips to the pet store to get things like a better harness and leash. He took Krystal to the groomer and asked if she would show him how to groom her. That young married woman liked Roger and knew how much he wanted to care for his dog himself. Over a few months time, she showed Roger how to groom Krystal. Then little Krystal had her very own personal groomer. That sweet small bundle of love was the inspiration to get Roger back to a healthier life.

chapter 17

GIFT OF TIME FOR MOTHER

Several years later, at the end of the time that Mother lived at the senior citizens' residence, she started to complain about the neighbors there. That was so unlike her. She never complained about anyone. So Roger and I discussed it and said we would offer to give her a place to live with us, again. Roger made arrangements to get Mother reestablished with the U.S. Government and she eventually got her citizenship papers. Those were happy days.

Mom spent a lot of time with Roger when he was resting. I was working the p.m. shift at Willow Point Nursing Home and this gave Roger and Mother the time to be together. When I slept after coming home from working the evening shift, I would awaken to the laughter of Mother and Roger. It thrilled my heart to know that they truly loved each other so. I was just about ready to retire. Mother would say, "I'll be so glad when you don't have to work any more. It will be so good to be with you." I was pushing to get to that time to spend more time with both Mother and Roger.

Mother came to live with us in Endecott, New York, in 1987. On May 9, 1991, Mother went up to her bedroom shortly after supper. I remained to finish cleaning up. When I came into her bedroom a while later I found her sitting in her rocking chair with the television on, but she was having a seizure. I called out to Roger, who was in our bedroom, to call 911. He came in but went into a state of shock himself when he saw her. I told him to stay with Mother, and I hurried to call for the ambulance. Within five minutes it arrived. I could hardly believe they were that fast.

Mother was taken to Sisters' Hospital in Johnson City. I went to the hospital by myself in our car, for Roger was in no shape to go. When I arrived at the hospital, Mother had been placed in a room by herself and intravenous medicines had already been started. I saw that she was still having seizures. Eventually I was able to leave Mother so I went into the waiting room. Its wide, high windows looked out over another part of the hospital, and clouds of steam filled the night air. Somehow the steam rising out of the building brought me comfort and gave me a sense that the Lord was with me.

At last Mother came out of the seizures. The next day was Mother's Day. I had purchased flowers and a gift for her as her doctor thought she could be discharged that Sunday. But on the day before, which was Sabbath, when I got to her room, she was not there.

The patient in the other bed told me that she had suffered another seizure and had been transferred to a different department on another floor. When I finally located her, spoke to her and touched her, she did not respond. She was in a coma. The coma lasted almost two months. I never saw any more seizures, but Mother did not regain consciousness. During some of my daily visits I thought perhaps she showed that she recognized me by tightening her hand in mine. Many times I remembered the words she had wistfully spoken—that she could hardly wait for me to retire. I had planned to retire soon. In fact, I officially retired the day after Mother was taken to the hospital with the seizures. But we never were able to realize her hope that we'd have more time together. I will always remember that.

A few weeks later, on this special Friday when I went to be with Mother as I had done every morning since she had entered the hospital, I met nurses bringing her back from X-ray. I asked why, but did not get any answer. That deeply upset me, and I determined then to bring her home and take care of her. I called Roger and told him what was happening, and he said he would be right down. The nurse knew I wanted to talk with my mother's doctor. She was in the hospital, so it worked out that I could see her. Roger had come, and when we went in to see the doctor, I explained that I wanted to take Mother home. She said that she would make arrangements with hospice and phoned them right then. The hospice leader was in the hospital and we made arrangements right there and then. Mother would be brought to our home on Monday. This was Friday.

At 7:00 o'clock Sunday morning I got a call that Mother had died. I called our son Daniel and he drove me to the hospital. When I entered her room the curtain was still drawn about her bed. I drew it aside and saw the airway tube still in her mouth. I could not believe such lack of consideration for the family. In the room across the hall from Mother was a priest, a patient there, and he called me over to see him. When I went to him he put his arm around me and said he was sorry that I had lost my mother. He was a frail, small man who was there for his own illness. He said, "I am so sorry about your mother dying, but you have been such a good daughter and have come here every day. God loves you."

It was a bright, beautiful morning. Daniel did not take me home but took me for a long, long drive in the country. We talked about many things. My heart was so comforted by this dear boy who himself was mourning the loss of his grandmother. That Daniel would think of me and my feelings and take the time to see that we were out in the lovely New York countryside among the tranquil sights of hills, trees, and sky, are memories I will never forget. When we finally drove to his home, his wife, Cheryl, was a comfort by hugging me. She was heavy with their second child, Adam—only a few weeks from delivery. God was wonderful to give us this new little life and to have given my mother to our family for so many years.

We had no service for Mother. We followed her desire to be cremated and buried in Niagara Falls, Ontario. Then Linda and Mike invited Roger and me to come to their home in in Modesto, California, for Thanksgiving and Christmas. This was in May, 1991, and we looked forward to seeing some of our kids at the holidays.

Daniel watched out for us after Mother died. One day he came with Muffins, a little kitten, that took more to Roger than to me. A few days after we got Muffins there was a terrible storm and we couldn't find her anywhere. We went to the garage and couldn't find her, looked under the bed and couldn't find her. I was very concerned but did not know what to do, so I finally stopped searching and got into bed. Still, I couldn't sleep. It was raining so hard I couldn't stop thinking about the kitten. So I got up, dressed again, and went outside, calling for Muffins up and down the block. No luck. I came back to the garage and for some reason went to the steps that led to the kitchen. There she was, her two little eyes looking at me. She was far back in a corner, mewing and frightened. I got her out, took her inside, and put her in bed with Roger and me where she went to sleep, purring. At that, I went to sleep too.

Another time Muffins was missing. Again I searched and searched for her. Finally I went to the poster bed and found that little Muffins had crept under the bed. There she was, right beneath Roger's head.

chapter 18

TWO PHONE CALLS

It was during the last years we lived in New York that a woman named Jodi Halstead contacted Roger, asking him to pray for her two daughters who were in prison in Oregon for murder. Roger learned more about their situation and did, of course, pray for them. However, he never thought that he would write the terrible story of how Seventh-day Adventist young adults were so deceived that they embraced spiritualism, actually obeying the commands of demon spirits.

Eventually Roger visited with Deborah Lynne and Sharon Lee in prison. He was unable to take notes from their conversations so when he decided to write their story he spent some years of labor to obtain the court transcripts. He knew all the facts of the story must be verified before he placed it where God could use it to lead His people to read and beware of the many ways Satan uses to deceive us. Strongly convicted that young people needed to be warned of the reality of the dark side, and that even Christians can be enticed away from the loving ways of God, Roger decided to write Deborah and Sharon's story. The book is titled *Beware of Angels*.

Roger received another phone call but this time it was a very positive experience. It was from Dan Houghton, president of Hart Research, who asked if it would be possible for him to come to our home in Endecott and record a filmed interview with Roger. The camera crew set up the tracks in our living room with lights both inside the house, and outside. Those lights shining through our windows got the attention of our neighbors who called to ask what was going on. We were somewhat embarrassed to tell them that Roger was the subject of an interview. The camera crew and guests were three young men and two wives who had come from Florida. It was October 11, 1991. What a time. Endecott in the fall is cold and crisp, the trees colors of every hue as winter approaches.

Krystal was put upstairs to allow Roger and Dan to speak without being interrupted, however, she kept whining, barking, and scratching to get out, no doubt, in her mind, to protect Roger. He finally asked Dan if they could let Krystal come and sit beside him during the interview for he was sure she would be quiet, and that is what they did. Krystal was happy—and so was everyone else!

When Dan Houghton learned of our trip out to California for the holidays, he made arrangements for us to go to Thousand Oaks, California, for more filming. Dan also interviewed Cyril and Cynthia Grosse at Thousand Oaks. They were instrumental in Roger's conversion from spiritualism. These exposures to a degree of fame among the church family were humbling times and brought a sense of God's willingness to use even Roger to help carry the love He is.

chapter 19

CALIFORNIA, HERE WE COME!

In 1991, the year Mother had died, we visited Linda and Mike in California. The weather was nice—nothing like upstate New York—and Roger felt so much better out there. He was less tired and was able to walk around the block. The children planted a little seed that we should move to California and that they would help us with the move. So in early April, 1992, our grandson, Michael, and our son-in-law, Mike, flew into the Bingington airport. Snow still covered the ground, and they soon realized how different New York weather was compared to California's. But it seemed like no time before our belongings were packed and we were on our way. The boys, Mike and little Michael, drove a Ryder Truck.

Roger and I spent that night with our son Daniel and his wife, Cheryl. I remembered how Daniel listened to our excitement of the trip, how telling him things we'd done and how much we had enjoyed it out there. Then with a choking voice, he said, "So, you have decided to move out West."

We suddenly realized we had not told him we were going to move. It broke our hearts when he told us how much he would miss us, but he understood that since Dad did so well there, the move would be for the best. Daniel is our youngest son, and we loved him and Cheryl so.

Saying good-bye to family and friends was not an easy task. Our hearts ached as we said our good-byes. My very precious friend, Susan, and I worked at Willow Point Nursing Home in Vestal, New York, she as an aide and I as an LPN. A dear friend loves at all times, good or bad. We had been parted six years earlier. This special day I was thinking of her and offered prayer for her and her family. We had not written or phoned each other for several weeks. Susan has to be one of the most thoughtful persons toward others I have ever known. Never a day went by that she wasn't doing something for somebody, making meals for shut-ins, shopping for those who no longer drove, taking care of neighbors' children, banking for shut-ins. You name it, if you needed help, she would be there for you.

Susan had had a difficult life. Her husband left her and three teenage daughters. She had a high school diploma, but no special skills. How was she going to handle their living expenses? She looked for work, and took on three different jobs to make ends meet. Susan was a terrific reader, interested in all subjects. She was so kind to the patients, giving them the best of care, always with a happy attitude. Susan was a faithful member of the Congregational Church where she taught a Bible class. She had read all of Roger's published books, and she loved the Lord as he did. When we talked with one another, we always thanked the Lord for all His blessings.

Now this is what happened. Shortly after I wrote the above paragraphs, Susan called me!

God made my day! Oh, how much He cares.

Roger did a lot of writing when we visited Linda and Mike. It was there where Roger started putting together the book, *Incredible Answers to Prayer*. When we arrived in California to live, we stayed with Mike and Linda for a year. They set up the dining room with Roger's equipment all around him, so he felt right at home soon after we arrived.

It was there that Roger experienced God's miracle copier. This is what he wrote about it.

"On March 8, 1991, I purchased a Canon-PC-1 Copier as a means of having copies on file of all letters that I write in reply to readers' prayer requests and inquiries. On December 10, 1993, while our grandson, Michael, was copying part of a book, the print cartridge ran out of toner. The operator's manual suggested turning the cartridge 90 degrees in both directions but that did not help. It was totally empty. There were no funds to get ink at that time."

Roger wrote of all the details in his book, but I will give a few highlights from the story. Roger had prayed that God would perform a miracle to make the ink cartridge continue and be a blessing for the work. Roger told God that he would tell of it and make sure everyone knew that this copier was performing because of God's power. He made a photocopy before the prayer, and it was so faint you could not see the words. After the prayer, the entire text of the photocopy came out clear and black. That copier worked without any purchase of ink for well over 22 months, making three times more photocopies than an ink cartridge normally produced. In his book *When You Need Incredible Answers to Prayer* (pps. 14, 15) Roger told the world how God performed a miracle for something only personally important to one of His children. He wrote: "About a month before, expecting the cartridge to run dry at any time, I had called several office supply stores to see where I would get the best price for a replacement.

The best price was $79 for a black ink cartridge (all other colors were more expensive).

"But now I was in a bind. On March 15, just five days away, we would move into our new apartment that had just cost me $1,200. We had paid the first month's rent and a security deposit of $300. In addition, we had put down $400 to cover any damage that our little dog and cat might do. (Hilda and I were learning that California is an expensive part of the world to live in.) As a result I realized that the copier would have to remain out of operation for at least a month before I would be able to spend any money on it.

"During the middle of that night I woke up and began counting my blessings and thanking God for the glorious ways His Holy Spirit was blessing the lives of so many people I had been praying for. As I prayed, a surge of joy flooded my heart and prompted me to ask the Lord a special favor. 'O Lord my God, if it be pleasing in Your sight would You please cause my copier to produce copies again? You know that I am on a limited income with no possibility of buying another ink cartridge for quite a while.'

"As Hilda and I had breakfast I told her about my conversation with the Lord in prayer and how I felt certain that we were going to see a manifestation of His creative power that morning. 'Why wait until breakfast is over to witness such a great blessing?' she said. 'Let's see it right now.' We went to the copier, turned the power on, placed a letter under the cover to photocopy, fed it a bright, white sheet of paper—and behold, a spotless copy came out at the other end. Praise to God filled our hearts."

To provide an author photo for each of Roger's books

he would go to have his picture taken. He would have me shampoo his hair. Roger was so handsome. He had such beautiful eyes. Many people would say "Oh, that salesman with the speaking eyes." And it was true, Roger had very expressive eyes. He was always happy and humming a tune. He had a happy heart. He loved life.

The hair shampooing didn't stop there. I washed his hair many times during our marriage. He would take a shower and wash it, but sometimes he would ask me to wash it instead. And I did. When we moved to Modesto, he went to a barber shop and the barbers were women. It was very close to where we lived, so Roger did not want to change barbers. When he'd come home, I would say, "Oh, honey, why did you have her cut your hair so short?" And he would agree that it was indeed short.

Then he returned from the barbers and his hair looked so nice. "Oh, darling, your hair's just lovely," I told him. "It's cut just right."

Then he said, "Well, I asked her to please not cut my hair so short. I told her that I'd give her extra money if she left it longer, because my wife does not like it cut too short."

Years later, when he was receiving letters from readers, many would say how depressed and unhappy they were. He would write and suggest that they pick out an uplifting hymn and sing it. If they'd do that, he assured them, God would bless and remove the depression in their minds. He received so many letters of this kind. His counsel was often the same, for them to find a hymn or a verse in the Bible that "you love, and these depressions will leave." If we start singing and humming, our hearts will follow and become happy.

As I mentioned before, we had met Elder Glen Coon

and his wife. Roger loved Elder Coon. He read his books on prayer and corresponded with the Coons. Elder Coon had come through darkness himself and knew the truth of what worked for his valley of depression—times when you cannot see any reason for living. In desperation, Elder Coon began to thank God for "the door that you can come through, the flowers that grow, the sunlight, the shadows, the air . . ." He found that gratitude was the antidepressant that cured his symptoms. My Roger practiced gratitude, always. Letters from Roger's readers testified to their gratefulness for depressions lifted when they did as Roger suggested. He always gave honor to God who lifted their hearts.

We lived with Linda and Mike for approximately a year. After that much time passed I'd look out at the garage and see all my own things, and *so* wanted to be in our own home again. One day I went for a drive. I had a craving for French fries and stopped at McDonald's. After receiving the fries I decided to go park on a quiet street to enjoy them. As I was eating the fries, a car pulled up about three or four houses from where I was parked, and a young woman with two small children got out and walked toward an attractive apartment house. So after I finished the fries I drove up the street and saw that the apartment house looked even more beautiful up close. The trees and the flowers were simply picturesque. Driving up to the entrance, I saw that the office was open. I immediately thought that I needed to go and talk with Roger. We'd talked before about renting an apartment, and Mike and Linda had taken us to some apartment houses, but we were not impressed with any of them. They were either too expensive or something else made them feel wrong for us.

When I got back home to Linda's, I said to Roger, "I think I have found a place we would like to live."

"Was the office open?" he asked.

"Yes, it is."

Roger said, "Let's go!"

When we got there, Roger was so impressed by how it looked from the outside. He went in by himself and eventually came out with one of the office girls and called to me, "Come on! We're gonna see an apartment."

Oh, how impressed we both were. It had two bedrooms on the same floor, and the price was within our reach. It was lovely—Stonebridge Apartments, 2800 Braden Avenue, Modesto. Our master bedroom was quite large, and Roger was able to set up his office there. The two bathrooms made it wonderful. We had a spare bedroom where many guests came and spent the night— Lorna Lawrence, Arlene Taylor, Mike and Luella Nelson, and other dear ones including Pastor Sherman, and Millie Jefferson. We were very, very happy. We even had an enclosed patio where we placed our bird feeders, a bird bath, and planted flowers. It was truly lovely.

Janet Page came to visit us in our apartment, and we came to love both Janet and Jerry Page who were new to their responsibilities, Jerry as president of the Central California Conference and Janet as women's ministries leader. Roger kept in touch with Jerry by phone with prayer needs for the conference, and Janet was faithful to let us know how things were going. Roger prayed often for these needs, knowing that God would answer and bless their ministries.

We lived at the Modesto apartment for five years, from 1993 until 1998 when Roger died. It was a perfect setting for the further work God had for Roger to do with his books. I still have the correspondence sent to Roger as well as his publication notes. He was very good at keeping these for reference to dates and details.

The experiences we had while we lived in Modesto remained in our memories. This particular event occurred one evening. Roger and I had been out grocery shopping, and when we returned, we parked our car and entered our apartment. Then Roger said to me, "Hilda, did you see that car that was parked out back?"

I hadn't seen it. But out back was a car with a man sitting in it. That was unusual. Shortly after we were in our apartment, we heard a knock on the door. It was early fall, the sun was setting, and it was already starting to get dark. Roger opened the door and the gentleman said to Roger, "Are you Roger Morneau?"

Roger said, "Yes. Come on in."

The man said, "I have driven for seven hours to come and see you."

I was busy putting the groceries away, but Roger invited him to sit down. This dear gentleman said to Roger, "I had to come and see this person who has written all these books on prayer."

It was a very strange experience. This man was so moved by coming to see Roger that he could barely speak. Roger did everything he could to make him feel comfortable. He did tell Roger that he was a physician, and he had many questions that he had prayed to God Roger would be able to answer for him.

Time was going on, and I realized we had not eaten supper. I went ahead and started fixing supper, knowing I would invite our visitor to eat with us. I could not hear all that was happening between Roger and this gentleman, but there were long periods of silence between the two of them. I think Roger was waiting on the Holy Spirit to tell him how to be helpful. The man was very troubled in his spirit.

He did participate with us in the meal, but there was little conversation at the table. It was a very, very sad kind of experience. We wondered what could possibly be troubling this person so deeply. He was so courteous and kind, apologizing in case he had inconvenienced us in any way.

I left the area then so the two men could be alone. Not too long after that our visitor said good-bye. He said he was going to drive back home now. Roger came in and said, "Honey, this man is so deeply troubled, but it seems he has found some peace here. Let's pray for him." We prayed.

We had another experience, also with a doctor. He had been corresponding with Roger, and in one of his letters he said he was going to come up with his wife and take us out to the Olive Garden restaurant. They were coming from Loma Linda. He was very impressed with Roger's method of praying and he himself had had many answers to prayer which he'd shared with Roger.

We went to the Olive Garden and enjoyed the meal and conversation. After we had eaten, the doctor left the table. We assumed it was to take care of the bill, but he did not come back. We kept watching for him. Fifteen minutes or so passed as we waited. Roger offered to get up to go and find out the problem. At last he saw the doctor coming back. "This is embarrassing," the man said, "but I have lost my wallet. We have been phoning all the places that we've been, including the inn where we slept this past night.

Roger said, "Don't worry about it. I can take care of this."

The man's wife said, "I will take care of it. I have money." They were so embarrassed. The doctor said, "Let my wife pay for it."

Roger told them that we needed to go back to the inn as he had strong feelings that it was somewhere in their room. The last time the doctor had seen his wallet was when he was in the bathroom. When we got to the inn, sad to say, we were told that the room had already been cleaned.

"I need to go into that room and see for myself," the doctor said. "May I get into it?" They let him go in. His wife, Roger, and I waited in the car, watching for him to come back. We were praying.

All of a sudden we saw him coming out—a wonderful, big smile on his face. He said, "Roger's prayers have been answered!" and told us this experience. He went through the suite, looking into the rooms, pulling out drawers, looking through the closets and bathroom. On his way out of the bathroom, heading for the door, his foot hit something. He bent down, and under the corner of the bed's quilted cover was his wallet! We all praised the Lord for being so good to us.

Arlene Taylor had been our 5-year-old friend when she was a child in Canada. Arlene's father, a pastor, is the one who married us. So several years ago when Arlene invited us to come to her place in Napa Valley for a weekend, we were delighted. We met Pastor Norman Doss and his wife, Florence, during that weekend, and became good friends.

Arrangements were made for us to go to Elmshaven—

the white two-story home where Ellen White spent her last years—for a private tour one Sabbath after church. Afterward we would go to the Doss's home for dinner. They had invited several other friends, and many pictures were taken. I recall that several pastors and doctors from St. Helena Hospital were there, and later went with us to the Doss's. At Elmshaven, we were in Ellen G. White's upstairs bedroom, where she did so much writing, when someone asked Roger to pray. We had come to love the writings of Mrs. White, and so this experience was precious to us. I don't think there was a dry eye in the room as Roger completed his prayer.

Pastor Doss kept in touch with Roger and me. He e-mailed Roger daily and kept him informed about the working of the Holy Spirit advancing Jesus' coming. He forwarded the articles from the Central California Conference that alerted Roger how to pray for the work.

When Roger corresponded with readers, he frequently did not dwell on the specific problem that their letters contained, but rather seemed to have one direction in his reply—to lead them to build up their faith in Christ, the Father, and Holy Ghost, our One God. There were the exceptions when a particular question was asked that Roger answered specifically. He knew he had no professional training or certification in guiding or counseling troubled people, and he freely shared this lack of professional background. Those who have read any of his writings will acknowledge his directing them to the Problem-Solver, Jesus, our precious Savior.

Many times I found Roger in prayer, bringing to God all whom he had committed to pray for as his own ministry, for the remainder of his life. By faith thousands upon thousands of names had been placed upon our Heavenly Intercessor's breastplate in the Heavenly Sanctuary where they will never be removed. Jesus brings these names before His Father in Heaven. Roger said on one occasion that if he had to be laid to rest, he would like for me to continue to pray for all those who came to us for prayer.

chapter 20

THE IMPACT OF
INCREDIBLE ANSWERS
TO PRAYER

There were times when looking through Roger's tattered and worn books after his death, that I longed to have his readers by my side to witness the love he had for the Word of God and his love for the gift God gave the Adventist church, the Spirit of Prophecy. Time and time again, I shed tears while reading passages of love and joy he'd shared with me, always making notes that he planned to use in his next manuscript. After Roger died, I found so many small pieces of paper tucked here and there throughout his materials, each with a quotation from the Bible or inspiring thoughts he was putting to memory.

When we went shopping and I was gathering up the things in the store, Roger would pick a certain spot to stay so I could find him when I was through. Roger really had patience. He never complained about the time it took to shop, for when I would finally join him I could see from a distance that he was enjoying himself by memorizing. He always kept a little piece of paper in his hand. This was a pattern he'd had since we married, well over 50 years before. He liked to rock from side to side as he memorized. I think that was part of the joy he experienced while he was memorizing. He loved his Lord with all his heart.

While we lived in Modesto, Roger got a call from Doug Batchelor asking if he and his wife, Karen, could come and visit with us. Of course we said yes, and I planned a luncheon meal for them. During the visit, Doug invited Roger to come to his church to be interviewed. Pastor Batchelor said that people in the congregation could ask questions, too. It was the Christmas holiday season, and I remember that the church was beautifully decorated. Doug read the questions, and Roger gave his answer.

The church was filled with people—sitting, standing, and others out in the lobby listening. Roger and I both were overwhelmed with how many people were there. Police officers were outside the building because there were cars parked everywhere. The questions dealt with many aspects of prayer and especially how to have the kind of relationship that Roger had with God where prayers were answered.

I recall the quote from Roger placed on the cover of *More Incredible Answers to Prayer:* "The Spirit of God has been transforming lives, remedying desperate conditions, and providing victory for the hopeless."

It is hard to express how much love many people had for Roger, and how much love Roger had for them. All he wanted to do was to help them know how personal and caring God is willing to be if they would just go to Him as they are, and allow Him to show them what to do. God, Himself, would give them the power to change into being His personal friend.

As the interview finished and Roger rose to leave the platform, elders rushed to his side to help him descend the stairs. They exhibited so much care for him.

Pastor Dwight Nelson called Roger to tell him that he had read his books and had put into practice some of his suggestions. They often conversed on the telephone.

Dwight said he was impressed with Roger's idea that we should daily read Matthew 27:24-54, which tells of the sacrifice of Jesus for humankind. In one of his sermons, Pastor Nelson told his congregation, "There is power in those words. IT works! It WORKS!" Roger called it the Power Chapter, and said that reading it daily would change the reader's life as the words revealed the depth of the love God had bestowed upon us through the giving of His Son. Roger recited those verses when he was interviewed by Doug Batchelor.

A few weeks before Roger died we were excited, planning to go to Michigan to attend "Net '98," a world-televised evangelistic series held in the large church where Dwight Nelson was senior pastor. He had invited Roger to offer the opening prayer.

Not everyone believed that Roger was genuine, or worthy of such attention. Neither did Roger think he was worthy of such attention, yet attention was given. Roger always took these negative attacks to the Lord, while his doctor repeatedly told him he was under too much stress. Though Roger practiced what he preached, leaving burdens with God, the demands upon his time were incessant. Because of world time differences, Roger received phone calls from all over the globe—England, France, Australia— at all different times of day and night. Many were from pastors who could not confide in their own peers so opened their hearts and concerns to Roger. Roger prayed seriously for each need, and knew that God would take the names and concerns and send the needed help for each one.

chapter 21

DARK DAY

I recall with such sweet memories how meticulously Roger had our things ready as we prepared for the trip to Andrews University at Berrien Springs, Michigan, for Net '98. By his bedside he kept the list of what we had to do before leaving: Pets—Krystal, our Schnauzer dog, went to Linda's, Jo-Jo and Muffins, our cats, went to pet boarding. Stop by the cleaners to get the suits. To take with us: medications, glasses, raw oats, protein (herbal powder), and personal care things. And, of course, take our Bibles and tickets. We were nearly all packed and ready to go.

Two days before we were to leave, the morning of September 22, 1998, in Modesto, Roger awakened me at 5:00 a.m. and said, "I don't know what is happening, but I don't feel well." I reached over and touched him. He felt cold though he was perspiring profusely. I quickly jumped out of bed and called 9-1-1. As I ran from the bedroom, he called out, "I'm going to be alright." But I hurried next door to my neighbor who was a nurse and asked her to come check on Roger.

She was already dressed for work at the hospital, and we both returned to Roger. By then he was unresponsive, and she could not get a blood pressure reading on him. In no time, the ambulance crew arrived and had Roger on the gurney and in the ambulance. I called my daughter,

Linda, and son-in-law, Mike, and they headed to Doctors Hospital. My mind was so distraught that I had not understood how I was to get to the hospital, so I waited for my family to come get me. After waiting for a time, I realized I'd only *thought* they were going to pick me up. I realized they'd gone directly there, so I got in the car and safely drove to the hospital on my own.

Mike and Linda were in the ER. They had not been able to see their dad. We waited and waited to hear any type of news. It seemed like eternity. Linda said that she would go to the cafeteria to get some drinks and when she got outside, she saw a friend, Mrs. Millie Jefferson, who was coming on duty at the hospital. Millie was earlier than she'd normally be, for she had to take a special nursing test where she worked on the maternity unit.

It was God-arranged for Millie to be there early. Pastor Herman Jefferson, Millie's husband, had been our pastor in Manteca, and she called him so he could come to be with us. When Pastor Jefferson heard about Roger, he tried to reach our Modesto pastor. He learned that the pastor was on his way to Walla Walla, Washington, as his children had been home from college for vacation, and he was taking them back. As we were waiting for Linda to come back, the ER nurse came and talked with us. She said that Roger had regained consciousness and told the staff working about him, "Get me off this cart. I'm going to be OK."

Hours later, the doctors came and told us that Roger's heart was so damaged there was no hope of saving him. We, as a family, had to make the heartbreaking decision to let him be at rest with the Lord. Roger and I had discussed the possibility of our facing such a decision—and now it had happened. It was now time to make the decision to take Roger off life support, no matter how difficult. So we did, and it was then that Roger died.

Afterward four or five pastors and elders came in and stood at Roger's side. I was there, too, for their special prayer of thanksgiving for his life and for comfort for his family. The children had not come in. Oh, such a sad moment! When Jesus returns and Roger is raised to life, he will shout, "Glory to God in the highest!" That was what Roger so often said when he was overjoyed by an answered prayer. At Christ's return, he will be his own vibrant joyful self, only better.

The notes and letters that poured in with love and sympathy for my loss of my lover and my friend were almost overwhelming. The following is taken from Dwight Nelson's letter and expresses the spirit of so many of the sentiments of the dear ones who wrote.

Dear Mrs. Morneau,

Our hearts have been deeply saddened over the death of your life companion, our friend, Roger. What a blessing he was to me, personally, through his writings and conversations, and what a blessing he has been to the world church.

I was stunned when Dan Houghton called last Tuesday evening with the word that he had died. And when I shared the sad news with our congregation here and our global satellite congregation, you could hear the audible exclamation of shock and sorrow. So many of us were looking forward to having you both in our midst for a few hours. . . .

chapter 22

THE YEARS
WITHOUT ROGER

Following Roger's death, the dear Doss family, Norman and Florence, visited often and were always there for me, encouraging and comforting. Then came the time in their lives when they decided to move into the Napa Valley Adventist Retirement Estates, at Yountville.

I recall that Pastor Luke Fessenden had come down to Roger's memorial service in Modesto. I met him again and his dear wife, Gerri—who were the managers of the Estates—when visiting the Doss's. It was Mike and Luella Nelson who made the plans for me to visit with Norman and Florence. I had such a happy time with these dear friends, and was very much impressed with their new home. Pastor Luke and Gerri gave me a tour. As yet I did not feel ready to move in, but I did put my name on the waiting list. Then I almost forgot about it.

One day I got a call that a studio apartment was now available. Only a couple of months previously, I'd had a car accident that totaled my car and shook me up. X-rays and more X-rays found no broken bones but I had enough bruises and muscular pain to be hospitalized for a few days. Yes, I soon came to the conclusion that it would be a good idea to join that beautiful home in Yountville.

Across the street was another beautiful building that had been such a joy to be part of, the Yountville Signs

Memorial Seventh-day Adventist Church. I loved being involved in their outreach programs. With others helping serve for the prisoners' children many Sabbath mornings, the Food-Give-Away program, helping with decorations for different events, volunteering for St. Helena Hospital, preparing and cleaning up after events—these were as important to me as the one other role Roger will certainly have a reaction to when he hears about it on Heaven's shore. I became one of the Yountville church's first women elders.

It was touch and go when the nominating committee for the 2006 officers asked me to be a church elder. In a church that had never had women in an elder position, this was major. I am not sure what Roger would have advised, but I know he would have prayed over it, as I did repeatedly. I prayed and earnestly studied the Word. My close friends encouraged me to accept, and I prayed on. It became clear to me that it would encourage the Yountville church if women were seen in leadership on Sabbath as elders and sometimes a speaker from the pulpit. I accepted the position along with Sue Alexander, one of the most talented of God's servants. The Lord has the plan, and I am eager to see it revealed to us when we are safely in Heaven. Roger might have said, "Go to it, girl!" or "Over my dead body!"

I do know I have grown with the Lord since Roger has passed, and he would be pleased to know how much I have trusted our Lord. May it ever be so, my prayer.

As I leave you, dear Reader, I long to see you in heaven where we can share notes of how our Savior and Friend has led us over the years. Roger had prayed for all those who had entrusted him with their prayer concerns, and when he was weaker, had asked God to never forget the many names that he held before Him. I know that this is the legacy each of us may leave, giving to God through prayer the ones we so love and the concerns we have. May your love and trust in God only grow stronger each day.

Roger would want your mind to be on God's inspired thoughts. As I leave you, here are two of our favorite passages giving us more understanding of the intimacy God desires for each of us, expressed in what Roger called, The Language of Heaven.

"Prayer is the answer to every problem in life. It puts us in tune with divine wisdom, which knows how to adjust everything perfectly. So often we do not pray in certain situations, because from our standpoint the outlook is hopeless. But nothing is impossible with God. Nothing is so entangled that it cannot be remedied, no human relationship is too strained for God to bring about human reconciliation and understanding; no habit so deep rooted that it cannot be overcome; no one is so weak that he cannot be strong. No one is so ill that he cannot be healed. No mind is so dull that it cannot be made brilliant. Whatever we need, if we trust God, He will supply it. If anything is causing worry or anxiety, let us stop rehearsing the difficulty and trust God for healing, love and power."[1]

"A person may not be able to tell the exact time or place, or to trace all the circumstances in the process of conversion; but this does not prove him to be unconverted. By an agency as unseen as the wind, Christ is constantly working upon the heart. Little by little, perhaps unconsciously to the receiver, impressions are made that tend to draw the soul to Christ. These may be received through meditating upon Him, through reading the Scriptures, or through hearing the Word from the living preacher. Suddenly, as the Spirit comes with more direct appeal, the soul gladly surrenders itself to Jesus. By many this is called sudden conversion; but it is the result of long wooing of the Spirit of God, a patient protracted process."

Thank You, Lord, for wooing me.[2]

[1]Ellen G. White, *Review & Herald*, October 7, 1865.
[2]Ellen G. White, *The Desire of Ages*, page 172.